TECHNO-ELEMENTALS

TECHNO-ELEMENTALS

© Copyright 2012-2018 David Spangler

All rights reserved. Except for the quotation of short passages for the purpose of criticism and review, no part of this publication may be reproduced, stored in a retrieval system or transmitted, in any form or by any means, electronic, mechanical, photocopying, recording or otherwise, without the prior consent the copyright holder and publisher. David Spangler has asserted his right to be identified as the author of this work.

Cover Art by Deva Berg
Edited by Julia Spangler

ISBN-13: 978-0-936878-59-1

Spangler/David
Techno-Elementals/David Spangler

First Edition March 2012
Second Revised Edition August 2018

Published by:
Lorian Press LLC
Holland MI 49424

www.lorianpress.com

TECHNO-ELEMENTALS

DAVID SPANGLER

ACKNOWLEDGEMENTS

The material in this book began as an experimental and exploratory class, evolved into an issue of my esoteric journal, Views from the Borderland, and now has become a book. In this process, I would like to acknowledge the many discussions and conversations on this topic I have had with those who participated in my class and in the online Forums based on the journal issue. Thank you, everyone, both for your willingness to join in the exploration and for your thoughts which helped sharpen my own.

I particularly want to thank my Lorian colleagues, Jeremy Berg and Timothy Hass, who have been road-testing these ideas in workshops of their design and my friend, John Matthews, who has been doing pioneering work in the shamanic exploration of cyberspace. They have all contributed deeply to the evolving understanding of these subtle beings who share our world with us.

I also want to thank my wife, Julia, without whose support and insights none of my work would be possible. Besides being my primary editor, she helps bring these concepts down to earth where they need to be.

Finally, I want to acknowledge with love and gratefulness my subtle colleagues who have been my own companions and guides into understanding the realms of the techno-elementals and other non-physical realities. There is so much more to discover and understand, but thanks to you, we have made a start.

CONTENTS

INTRODUCTION 1
FIELD NOTE 1: THE SPECTRUM OF LIFE 5
FIELD NOTE 2: A SUBTLE ECOSYSTEM 13
FIELD NOTE 3: A LIVING UNIVERSE 16
FIELD NOTE 4: A LEARNING UNIVERSE 22
FIELD NOTE 5: THE EIGHT FUNCTIONS 26
FIELD NOTE 6: ARTISANAL FORCES 32
FIELD NOTE 7: ELEMENTALS 38
FIELD NOTE 8: NATURE SPIRITS 44
FIELD NOTE 9: THE ANATOMY OF AN ARTIFACT 48
FIELD NOTE 10: TECHNO-ELEMENTALS 60
FIELD NOTE 11: FROM TALISMAN TO TECH 72
FIELD NOTE 13: FRANKLIN'S KEY 79
FIELD NOTE 13: THE GRAIL OF EVOLUTION 86
FIELD NOTE 14: THE BROKEN BRIDGE 92
FIELD NOTE 15: DIMMING 98
FIELD NOTE 16: SOOT 105
FIELD NOTE 17: ECHOES 112
FIELD NOTE 18: SHAZAM! 118
FIELD NOTE 19: ROOMIES 125
FIELD NOTE 20: CYBERSPACE, ROBOTS, AND AI, OH MY! 134
FIELD NOTE 21: PARTNERSHIP 139
EXERCISES 142

DEDICATION

I dedicate this book to all who seek to bring love into our world, to bless the life in the things we make, and thereby manifest wholeness for all creatures on the earth, physical and subtle.

INTRODUCTION

When I was eighteen, my father bought me my first car so that I could drive back and forth from college. It was a four-year old, 1959 Chevy Impala that had belonged to my cousin. It was at the time one of the most popular cars in America, possessing a distinctive sleek look with tailfins that flared horizontally outward rather than upward.

It had been a reluctant purchase, though. My Dad was a protective father, and the idea of me behind the wheel out in traffic where anything might happen gave him nightmares. It wasn't that he doubted my driving skills. It was all the other "damn fools on the highway" that gave him pause. Having lived through my two sons and two daughters becoming drivers, I can now understand the worries that can grip a father's heart when his children first begin to navigate the highways, but at the time, his fears both amused and frustrated me.

Where Dad was concerned, my car had two strikes against it. The first was that it was *my* car, and I was driving it rather than being safe on a bus or with him behind the wheel. The second was that it wasn't a Volkswagen Beetle. Dad had only owned Beetles since we returned from Morocco in 1957, and he thought this unique-looking German car was about the best in the world. However, Dad had gotten a very good deal on the Impala from my cousin who had practically given it to us as a favor to me; financially, he'd been unable to pass it up.

I loved my car. Frankly, at that point in my life, I would have loved any car that I could call my own, but the Impala with its impressive tailfins was, I felt, just about the coolest car on the road. It was my spaceship!

My Dad, though, disliked it thoroughly and saw it as a necessary evil. This led to an interesting turn of events. When I drove the car by myself, everything worked perfectly. I never had any trouble with it. That car and I had a love affair going, and the purr of its engine as I drove along the highway was like angels singing.

However, whenever my Dad got in the car with me, or, more rarely, attempted to drive it, something always went wrong. It was always a little thing, some rattling here or some knocking there; maybe a window didn't work right, or the car would momentarily stall when he tried to start it up. It was never enough to put it in a garage, but it was something annoying. Dad concluded that the car was a piece of junk, which only increased his worrying when I drove it.

I was intrigued by this phenomenon and laughingly told Dad that the car didn't like him because he was hurting its feelings. It was a joke, but the more it happened, the more convinced I became that something like that was going on. So, I investigated.

I have always been able to perceive beyond the range of the five senses into what I call the "subtle" dimensions of the world. Here I find a non-physical ecosystem every bit as diverse and rich as the one we see in the physical world around us. Further, this subtle ecosystem overlaps and integrates in a variety of ways with our material universe. Objects that appear inert and non-living to us with our physical senses may be filled with life in the subtle realm. The experience of the universe as fully and totally alive was well-known to our ancestors; it's only within the past three hundred years or so, since the beginning of the Industrial Revolution, that our Western society has forgotten this in its exclusive focus upon material reality.

I think of this subtle world with all its diversity and interconnectedness as Earth's "second ecology." It's deeply woven into and interdependent with the physical ecology with which we are familiar. We ignore this "second ecology" to our detriment, especially at a time when we need to find ways to reestablish and reaffirm our wholeness with our planet. To think and speak of the subtle realms merely as fantasy or folklore, as the supernatural or mystical, is to misunderstand its nature and to blind ourselves to the richness and gifts of life which it offers.

When I looked into the subtle energy fields around my car, I did find a being that had integrated itself into those fields. My car had become a link for it with the physical world and even more importantly, with the human world. At the time, I did not have enough experience to understand what this meant or why it might be important. I simply knew that there was a consciousness surrounding and permeating my car that responded in one way to my love and appreciation for it and another way to my Dad's dislike. For me, it worked perfectly. For my Dad, it created problems. Not so different from how people react!

This was my introduction to the species of subtle beings I have come to call "techno-elementals." These are subtle beings that align themselves with human technology and artifacts. Fifty years later, I decided to write about them.

I have written two books on the subtle worlds—*Subtle Worlds: An Explorer's Field Notes* and *Working with Subtle Energies*. I also write an esoteric journal, *Views from the Borderland*. This journal, published four times a year by the Lorian Association, provides me with an opportunity to share my observations, experiences, and communications from encounters and explorations of the subtle realms. These are my personal "field notes," and through them, I seek to introduce people to the reality, the wonder, and the naturalness of the non-physical world around us.

In 2012, I dedicated the fourth issue of this journal to the topic of techno-elementals. This volume was only available to those who subscribed to my journal that first year of its existence and has never been sold to the general public. Yet, given the importance of techno-elementals in our lives, the information it contains deserves a wider audience, I believe. Therefore, I'm happy to offer another exploration of these beings in this book, with new material not present when I first wrote about them in my journal.

I always begin each issue of *Views from the Borderland* with the following caveat: *All the following material is based on my personal observation. While I present it as accurately and clearly as I am able, it is subject to the limitations of my own experience, understanding, bias, perceptual abilities, and skills of interpretation. While I have years of experience in this area, I am most certainly not infallible. I am still exploring and learning. Another person, making the same contacts or observing the same phenomena as I, might have a different perception or a different interpretation and understanding. This being said, I invite you to join with me in exploration. If anything here resonates with your mind and heart, may it be a blessing and a help to you.*

This is especially true of this book. It should be seen as part of an ongoing exploration, a beginning venture into understanding the nature of some of the subtle beings that share our lives with us. To this end, each chapter is a "Field Note," an observation I've made, and not in any way the final statement on the subject. In all respects, this book is only a beginning, first steps in exploring a specific aspect of the vast, complex, and wondrous ecosystem of the subtle realms. I hope it will be helpful in encouraging and assisting further exploration and discovery.

Because of the nature of the material, this is a book of esoteric ideas and concepts, many of which may be unfamiliar to you. I have tried to keep things as simple as possible while still covering the territory and providing insights into the nature of the beings in question. I have felt the need to go into as much detail as I've been able to perceive. But if you find this to be more detail than you want, please feel free to skip ahead to Field Note 19, "Roomies." It, plus the Exercises and Examples at the end, contains the practical, "how-to" information of what we can do in relationship to the techno-elementals in our lives, which, after all, is the most important thing to know!

FIELD NOTE 1: THE SPECTRUM OF LIFE

When I was six years old, my parents and I went to see a movie that included a Walt Disney cartoon. In this animated short feature, the furniture and other objects were all alive and talked to the characters. I remember sitting in the dark watching this, thinking, "Someone's made a movie about *my* world." Not that in the world I experienced sofas and chairs got up and sang and danced as they did in the Disney cartoon (which, I must admit, would have been pretty cool) or carried on extended conversations with me, but they definitely had a presence, a sentient energy of which I was aware. And interaction between me and that sentiency was possible.

The idea that everything is alive has been part of the shamanic world view for millennia and in more recent history can be found in some religious mystical traditions as well. The pervasiveness of life is something individuals in all cultures and times have experienced. Even in popular language and culture, we invest our things with personalities and talk about them as if they were alive. Modern science and psychology would say this is merely anthropomorphic projection on our part, but older wisdoms would see this differently. And now there are branches of complexity theory and the science of nonequilibrium thermodynamics that are broadening our definition of what is life beyond the boundaries of biology and organic chemistry.

As shamanic ideas have become more present in our culture, particularly among those who explore and practice alternative and nature-oriented spiritualities, and we have become more holistically and ecologically minded, the phrase "Everything is alive" is bandied about more commonly. But what exactly does it mean? What is this life that everything shares? A mystic might say that it's God's Life or "Universal Life," but just what does that mean when applied to metal and plastic or to my favorite sofa? No one, I think, would claim it's the same as the life that animates you and me, the birds outside my window, or the trees in which they are nesting.

Yet all my life I have experienced everything around me as alive.

life to me is not just a biological or organic phenomenon. It is an energy manifestation that is organized and self-sustaining, an eddy or vortex within a larger flow of universal energy. What does this mean?

Let me give you an example of how I experience the presence of life within an inanimate object, something normally considered unliving. For this purpose, I choose a sofa in my living room.

My sofa, like everything else in the world, is onion-like. It's a collection of layers of being, which, falling back on metaphors from physics and electromagnetism, I think of as different "frequencies." I could think of it like a radio which plays multiple stations, each broadcasting on a different wavelength. To listen to a particular station, I have to tune in to the frequency of its broadcast.

To confess, I don't like this word, *frequency*, to describe what I perceive of the different "layers" in which life manifests. It's too "electronic" an image and doesn't capture the vibrancy and sentiency of what is there. Maybe "dimensions of being" would be more accurate. But frequency has the advantage of being a single word that most people recognize, so I'll continue to use it, though with caution.

With this in mind, my sofa has different "broadcast frequencies" ranging from the concrete, physical level of atoms, molecules, and material substance all the way to the most primal, universal "frequency" of all, that of the Sacred, the One Beingness that pervades all creation. I don't know how many of these frequencies or dimensions of being constitute the total phenomenon I think of as my sofa; I can't perceive or tune in to all of them. But I'm aware of several of them. Let me describe the ones of which I *am* aware.

The first thing I see when I look at my sofa is what anyone would see: its surface appearance. It's a tad over seven feet in length, just perfect for lying down on to watch television. It's made of wood and cloth and a thick padding, with equally thick, soft cushions. It's ivory in color. It's lovely to look at and very comfortable. And at this level of perception, it's very ordinary and not at all "living" in any normal sense of that word.

If I shift my awareness and perception, at the first frequency beyond the physical, the sofa becomes something more. I am aware of an energy field surrounding the physical form of the sofa. This field is "sticky" and can accumulate other "bits and pieces" of subtle energies, such as those generated by our thoughts and emotions. For example, if I'm content and peaceful when I sit or lie upon the sofa, the vibration of that peace can enter this energy field and stick there, at least for a time; likewise, if I'm agitated and upset, those emotional energies can be caught. It's as if there's a layer of psychic Velcro around the sofa that catches and holds energetic "lint" from the mental, emotional, and spiritual activity in the environment.

If these psychic energies are repeated over and over, they can become deeply impressed upon the energy field of the sofa, going more deeply into its energetic substance than just this surface "Velcro" layer I'm describing. But otherwise, this energy "lint" is lightly held and can easily be removed through some practice of energy hygiene or cleansing. Just doing one's housework with love and in a cheerful manner—especially with the vibration of music—while visualizing clean, clear, vital energy sweeping through the room and the furniture can usually wipe such stuff away. (For a more in-depth treatment of energy hygiene to deal with this psychic "lint," please see my book, *Working with Subtle Energies*.)

Feeling this trapped subtle energy can give a psychic impression of something life-like, I have found, but it's really the life energy of others "recorded" on the subtle substance of the sofa. At this simple level, the sofa is energetically active, as most things are, but this is not the same as being alive. To discover how life itself inhabits my sofa, I must go deeper.

In astronomy, there's a concept called *the habitable zone* which is the distance from a star at which a planet could have conditions favorable to the existence and evolution of life such as we know it. How large this zone is and where it is found in a solar system depends on the nature and characteristics of that system's star. (Astronomers sometimes call this the "Goldilocks Zone" because it's neither too hot nor too cold but "just right.")

In a similar way, when I look for the life within the sofa, I look for a "Goldilocks Energy Zone" in which the universal flow of life becomes organized to form patterns energy that are persistent and self-sustaining to some degree. To me, such patterns are all *incarnational* systems. They don't just accumulate energy or substance; they organize it in some persistent manner; they are *autopoietic* or self-producing. They possess some level of coherency and integration. In my terminology, they possess *identity* which creates a boundary of some nature that separates them from the rest of the energy flowing around them.

Imagine a river. As it flows, a branch lies across the river bank and into the water, and where it dips into the river, it impedes or restrains that flow to some degree. The water becomes turbulent in the area around the branch; an eddy may form. This eddy is a shape, a presence that persists even though water flows through it as long as the branch is there forming a boundary to catch that flow.

If the river is the flow of living energy from the Generative Mystery we call the Sacred, then one manifestation it produces is like that eddy, a complex organization of flowing energy in and around a boundary condition that defines its particularity and enables a system of organization to develop and persist.

As I examine my sofa with a deeper perception, I come to this pattern of organized living subtle energy that is not just an accumulation of "energetic lint" from outside itself. It is an energetic presence that has its own unique, internally coherent and integrated organization. This is where I experience the sofa as something living, not in a biological way certainly but as a unique configuration of sentient energy.

What is this life like as I perceive it?

To use the metaphor of the river again, the branch that produced the eddy of energetic organization in this instance is the human imagination that created the sofa. This creative imagination forms a framework of intent around which energy begins to organize itself. It provides the matrix for a pattern of living energy to take form associated with the physical form of the sofa.

The energy pattern of the sofa at this "Goldilocks" level doesn't look to me like a sofa at all. In fact, it doesn't "look" like anything in particular in the way that we are accustomed to physical objects having forms; rather it is a "shape of consciousness" that reflects the potentials of interaction held and defined by this pattern.

Sentiency is an important key here. My friend Dr. Lee Irwin, a religious scholar and mystic and the author of many books on spirituality, defines sentiency as "the impulse to form relationship." Relationships and connections are the foundation for manifesting wholeness, and manifesting wholeness is what creation is all about, from my point of view.

The "consciousness-shape" of the living energy field around the sofa possesses this sentiency (which is not the same thing as what we experience as conscious awareness); it is organized to sense and form energetic connections and relationships in a unique manner as defined by its pattern. It is this coherent organization that is the life of my sofa, it's "incarnational" pattern.

When I experience this "energetic shape" that is my sofa, it is not terribly complex or flexible; it does not possess initiative, for instance. A human being, by comparison, is immensely more complex, organized, and capable as an energy form.

To introduce a new metaphor, toy action figures are classified by "points of articulation," that is, by the joints that they possess which determine where they can bend and how flexible they are. As a kid, I had a set of plastic toy soldiers that were each molded as a single piece. They had no points of articulation and could not bend at all. Later I had toy soldiers that had one point of articulation; they could bend at the waist. In time, toy manufacturers made figures that could turn their heads or move their hands or feet, their elbows or knees. They had more points of articulation, more joints, and the more they had, the more they could be posed in the various positions that a real person could take. You didn't have to imagine that your toy soldier was kneeling or bending or sitting; he really could kneel, bend, or sit.

Human beings energetically have an immense number of "points of articulation" or "joints of sentiency;" these are the many ways our consciousnesses can "bend" and configure to the environment, take initiative, create, and so on. My sofa has only a few joints of sentiency, and thus it is much more limited as an energy presence than I am in what it can perceive and do. Yet it is not totally unaware or inanimate at this energetic level.

I experience this every day, not just with my sofa but with all the objects around me. They all possess a field of living energy and sentiency at this "Goldilocks" level. If I send an energy of love or appreciation to them, they respond. It's like blowing upon a coal which then brightens and flares up with heat and light. A connection is made, and there is a flow of love back to me. Over time, this relationship can become etched into the subtle energy environment, like a groove or a path across the land where the land is beaten down by the passage of many feet over time.

So, I discover that at a certain level or frequency of energy, a structure of sentiency and responsiveness exists in my sofa. It is this organization of sentiency that I experienced as a child and felt as the life within the furniture and other objects that made up my world, so charmingly and whimsically portrayed in the Disney cartoon.

Under the right circumstances, something else may occur, one intimately connected with the phenomenon of techno-elementals. The energy pattern around an object may become a point of contact and connection for a different non-physical entity which itself may be significantly more advanced and aware. If this were to happen to my sofa, then when I tuned into it, I might find myself in contact with a spiritual being that would be quite capable of engaging and communicating with me. This being would in effect be a "rider" on the energy of the sofa, though operating at a different frequency.

When my first child was five, we took a trip to Disneyland where I bought him a stuffed animal. It was Bumblelion, a creature that was part bumblebee and part lion, the star of a popular Disney cartoon series on television at the time. It was so whimsical and cute, I couldn't resist it, and John-Michael fell in love with it. It went everywhere with him; it became his constant companion whether he was playing, eating, or sleeping.

One day I was holding Bumblelion and became aware of a presence around it. As it turned out, it was a kind of playful spirit that was also partly a protector. It was one of a class of beings—I suppose one could think of them as angels—that regularly associate with children.

This one had attached itself to the energy field of this toy. Johnny had poured so much love into this stuffed animal that its own energy organization had become more complex. Its sentiency, its capacity to form relationship, had been heightened, enough that this inner being could see it and connect to it. It was using this toy as a point of physical connection to our world through which its own loving and protective energies could flow.

After that, when I would buy a stuffed animal for one of my children or for the children of friends, I would make a point of energizing the toy with love and then reaching out to one of these beings to invite it to connect with that energy and make that toy a point of contact to better bless the child who would be using it. Stuffed talismans!

I want to be clear that such beings do not inhabit the object; they are not "possessing" it (like an evil doll in the movies). They are simply forming a link through which a level of engagement with and participation in our world is possible, but the participation is not through the instrumentality of the object. It's through their own energy field in relationship to our own.

I picture this sometimes as a diver wearing a weighted belt to overcome his own buoyancy so that he can remain submerged. The frequency of energy on which many beings operate makes it challenging to directly be present to our physical realm; they are energetically "too buoyant." But linking to the energy field of one of our objects gives them "weight," so to speak. It's not an exact metaphor; most physical metaphors fall short of adequately or accurately describing the reality of subtle phenomena. But hopefully, it gives a sense of what is happening, as it is important to understanding the nature and functioning of "techno-elementals," the topic of this book.

There's a final thing I want to share. There is a dimension of consciousness, a "frequency" of life, within my sofa—and within all things, ourselves included—that I could say lies at the very "bottom" or the very "top," whichever you wish. It is foundational. In seeking to tune in to the "Goldilocks" layer of life within my sofa, it's possible I may "overshoot" the mark and find myself slipping into a mystical state in which I become aware of a Presence and Life that is not just within the sofa but within all things. This is the primal Life from which all creation is emerging, what I think of as the level of the Sacred. This Life is a universal condition. It's the Life we all share, the Life of the Cosmos, the Life of the One, however we may conceptualize that.

At this level, the sofa is most definitely alive, but it's no longer a sofa. Nor is it a distinct, organized energy field, with its own boundaries and characteristics. At this level, the energy I sense, the life I sense, is part of a universal oneness flowing through all things, underlying the manifestation of all things. It is the river from which the individual eddies and vortices of manifestation and creation are formed. The Cosmos itself is alive. There is really nothing more to say about it than this, though the implications are profound.

What I want to share here is that we can see life as a spectrum. What we think of as "life" is really only a thin slice of that spectrum, just as what we see as visible light is only a small fraction of the whole electromagnetic spectrum. There are multiplicities of diverse forms that life takes in the physical world; this is even more true when we consider the non-physical or "subtle" side of things. From where we are on this spectrum in our consciousnesses and energy, there are forms of life much simpler than our own, such as the life within my sofa, and there are forms of life infinitely more complex than our own, such as the life of the Planetary Angel we call "Gaia."

Techno-elementals exist within the subtle frequencies of this spectrum in ways that intimately connect to our own. This is what we will explore in the field notes to come.

FIELD NOTE 2: A SUBTLE ECOSYSTEM

To understand techno-elementals, we need to think in new ways. If you've never considered the reality of the subtle worlds, doing so may be a stretch into unfamiliar territory. I would like you, though, to take another, further step with me. This is to think of the subtle realms as an ecosystem and subtle beings as organisms, terms normally restricted to biological life and its relationships with its environment.

In my experience, life is life wherever we find it or however it manifests. All organisms, whether they're cows, trees, dogs, bacteria, people, nature spirits, Devas, or angels, exhibit similar characteristics and obey certain principles. All manifest an identity and an associated coherent field—a "body"—through which they can express that identity. That body may be of a substance altogether different from that of physical matter and may look like nothing with which we are familiar in the physical world, but it's a body nonetheless. All beings exchange energy with their environment. All to some extent shape and are shaped by their environment. All possess means of connecting and interacting with others; all communicate, though not necessarily in any way we would recognize or understand. All possess sentiency. All possess a capacity for change, development, and learning, which is to say, all embody intelligence, even if in a form wholly unlike that which we humans demonstrate.

A friend steeped and trained in Zen Buddhism once said to me, "You know, David, in the Zen tradition, subtle beings, even if real, are considered distractions on the path to enlightenment. We are taught to ignore them." I understand the sentiment. He was pointing to the glamour, such as fear or excitement, around encountering something that many people deem supernatural. This glamour can be distracting.

The problem my friend brought up is about more than simple distraction. Anything can be distracting. The issue is the way we think about the non-physical dimensions, the images and words we use. For a very long time, humanity has viewed them as a separate and basically unknown, even fearful, reality, the province of religion, magic, mysticism, and superstition. They are the realms of the dead, of spirits and ghosts, of nature forces, and gods and goddesses, powers beyond human ken, best left alone by ordinary people.

But for me, the subtle realms are not "supernatural." They are "differently natural." They are an extended part of the ecology of a planet that is much vaster than just its physical parts. Although they are formed from subtle energies that have much in common with what we experience as thought, feeling, and spirit, they are as much a part of the natural order of things as forests or mountains, oceans or rivers. We just have too narrow a view of what constitutes "natural."

A fuller exploration and explanation of what I like to call "Earth's second ecology" is beyond the scope of this little book, which has a more specific focus. I refer you to other volumes in my Subtle World series if you are interested.

The point I wish to make here is that we will understand the nature of techno-elementals better if we can see them as organisms of mind and energy who are drawn to us for reasons that would make sense to any living creature because we have something to offer them that can benefit their lives. In the process, they become an influence in our lives, sometimes in positive ways and sometimes in ways that can be dangerous if we fail to appreciate their nature.

Where I live in the Pacific Northwest, crows are everywhere. For years now, two crows have nested nearby and show up on my porch almost every morning. The reason is simple. I like to feed them. I'm not trying to tame them or turn them into pets; I doubt that I could. They view me with a wary familiarity, and I know they know they have nothing to fear from me. I have no motive other than to bring some pleasure into their lives because their presence also brings me pleasure. They are beautiful birds.

I am hardly a "crow whisperer." I have no doubt the crows would ignore me if I didn't put food out for them. I'm very sure they wouldn't land on my porch or, as one crow sometimes does, land on a chair on the porch that's next to the kitchen window and peer in to see if I'm around and what I'm doing, letting me know he's out there. They would have no reason to interact so closely to my human world if it didn't hold something of interest and, even more, of nourishment for them.

The beings that are techno-elementals are much like my crows. They enter our human world because it holds something of value to them. They are doing what organisms do. In so doing, a relationship may be set up that can benefit all concerned. This is what I wish to explore with you in this book. This exploration begins with appreciating that we are dealing with lifeforms, organisms, that deserve the same love and respect that we would offer to any living creature in our world. For they *are* part of our world. It's just that the world is larger and more wondrous than most people suspect.

FIELD NOTE 3: A LIVING UNIVERSE

I was taking an afternoon walk in my neighborhood. It was one of those rare days in the American Pacific Northwest when the sky was clear and the sun was shining, and there were no clouds to obscure its face. It had been a long and enjoyable walk in the sunshine, but I was ready to get home. Coming to a corner and seeing my house a block away ahead of me on the other side of the street, my thoughts were already turning towards the things I had yet to do that day. I hardly noticed I was passing a lovely row of flowers that a neighbor had planted between his front lawn and the sidewalk on which I was walking.

I was about to cross the street when I felt a tap on my right shoulder as if someone were trying to get my attention. I stopped and looked around and saw a small being, about four feet in height, appearing in the midst of the row of flowers. I'm often aware of the subtle energies of nature spirits in the landscape around me, but rarely does one of these beings appear in such a distinct, visual manner, looking very much like a small human. As I stood there, looking at it in mixed surprise and delight, it smiled, reached out and tapped my arm again with one hand and pointed upward with the other. It obviously wanted me to look up, so I did.

There, high in the blue sky above me, was a wide ribbon of golden light running east and west. I had no way of judging its size as there was nothing I could see with which to compare it. Nor did I have any sense of its height, though it seemed to me to be several hundred feet up. It was undulating, and, I realized as I watched it, it was floating down, not exactly like a cloud or a mist—it was too well-formed for that—but more, I thought, like a huge, long, golden blanket descending upon the earth.

I stood there trying to understand what I was seeing. As I did so, I caught a fleeting inner glimpse of a vast and loving shining Presence—a Deva, perhaps—who was the source of this phenomenon.

I looked back at the nature spirit, but it was gazing up at the sky with anticipation and joy on its face. I then realized that there was a feeling of similar anticipation and excitement rippling through the subtle environment around me.

Looking back up, I was aware that the golden ribbon of light and energy was closer to the earth now, and I could see that it was going to cover most of the valley in which I live, including the nearby lake. As it descended, I could feel the subtle life around me in the neighborhood seem to open and reach up to receive it. I asked the nature spirit what this was, what was happening. This was not a being accustomed to communicating with humans and certainly not by using words. What came was a mélange of images and impressions, all suffused with joy. As best I could translate it, this golden ribbon was a downpouring of blessings from a generative Source of Light in a higher realm of life. I was not sure whether this was a regular occurrence every day or something special—time was meaningless to the being who was communicating with me. What was evident, though, was that this energy represented a form of nourishment.

As the "blanket" of energy descended, it seemed to me to turn into a fine, golden mist that covered the neighborhood. The small being standing next to me grew visibly brighter as this happened, before it faded from my view. I knew from past experiences that these beings would in turn help the plants, the minerals, and the soil around me absorb the qualities offered by this blessing of subtle life-force.

I have no idea if what I saw clairvoyantly that afternoon as the golden blanket of Light and energy is how the nature spirit who alerted me to its presence saw it. I'm quite sure I didn't connect to that energy in the way it did. It was not "food" for me, at least not in the same way. I could have been watching a farmer spreading out oats and hay for her horses. Yet it certainly left me with a sense of the love, the joy, and the caring that permeates the subtle realms of nature.

Though this experience was singular in the visual form it took, it's theme was not unusual for me. There is a being that overlights the lake in our valley. I am often aware of currents of life-force, energy, and blessing radiating out from her over the surrounding land, bringing nourishment of its own kind to the various subtle lives—and,

I believe, the physical ones as well—who are part of this environment. Similarly, I'm aware of the Light and energies radiating from the Deva overlighting Mt. Rainier, some fifty miles or so to the south. These are only two of many currents of nourishing energies permeating the subtle environment, originating from a wide variety of sources.

The subtle ecology is an active, alive place. Within it are certain discernible—I would even say, universal—activities, which the story I just related helps to illustrate.

The first of these is what I call **Holding**. This activity holds the boundaries and energetic structure of a particular manifestation such as a tree or a stone, or for that matter, of a sofa or a lamp. Of course, the physical structure of a plant is determined and maintained by well-known botanical and biological features, and my sofa's physical structure is a product of its manufacture and is held together by principles of physics and chemistry. But in the subtle worlds, boundaries and structures are more fluid and are manifestations of intent and energy. In addition, there is a cross-over between the subtle and physical worlds. It is a well-documented phenomenon that directed thought can alter the physical structure and behavior of a plant. Plus the ability to affect the physical body through subtle means is at the heart of energy healing or healing through prayer and blessing.

The fact is that healthy subtle energies are active; molding that activity into coherent, integrated energy fields and forms with functional boundaries is what the activity of Holding is all about. In my story, the roses by the sidewalk all had their own subtle intelligence and inner life that held intact the subtle energetic component of what enabled them to be roses and not, say, daises or sunflowers.

A second important activity is **Generativity**. All subtle beings are generative to one degree or another, but many subtle beings, especially those we call angels and Devas, generate nourishing and empowering subtle forces as a distinct and deliberate function. Just as the sun supplies energy to power our planetary ecology and its life in the physical world, so there are beings in the subtle worlds who are generative sources supplying subtle energies that empower life and activity in the non-physical realms.

The golden blanket of energy that I saw apparently descending from the sky (though in fact it was precipitating out from a higher frequency of Life) had been generated by the being whom I had glimpsed. I thought it was a Deva, perhaps the overlighting "Landscape Deva" of the valley in which I live, but the contact was too brief to be sure. My assumption was based on the fact that this is what many Devas do, using their generative powers to "feed" other forms of subtle life.

It may well have been, though, that the true source of the energy I witnessed was on a plane of being higher than I could perceive and that the being I saw was not generating it as much as circulating it, making what had been generated more widely available. This would highlight the third activity, that of **Circulation**. In effect, this means taking energy from one being and passing it on to another.

I can draw a clearer example of this from my backyard. My maple tree has its own spirit, an Intelligence that holds its energetic identity and integrity. However, I can at times discern around the tree small, shining beings that I think of as nature spirits. They are actively receiving nourishing subtle energies from various sources and translating those energies into a form that can be absorbed by the energy field of the maple tree. In effect, they are circulating life energies that support the tree energetically in its holding.

This is what the small nature spirit that alerted me to the downpouring of subtle energies was doing. It was receiving what had been given and was passing it on in a form the environment around it could receive and absorb. In this sense, such beings might also be understood as "agents of absorption," enabling a subtle organism busy with holding the energy field of its manifestation to receive and take in subtle energies it might not otherwise be able to assimilate. A biological equivalent could be those bacteria that take free nitrogen and "fix" it chemically in the soil in a form that a plant's roots can take in and make use of.

The subtle environment as I experience it manifests synergy. It is filled with beings of different kinds and functions, forming connections, engaging with each other, circulating life-stimulating subtle energies between them, and creating in their collaborations a wholeness that is greater than just the sum of its parts.

In so doing, subtle beings are continually forming and supporting relationships, and relationship is foundational to the creative process. No being is meant to exist in isolation; we are all part of ever-expanding networks of participation, relationship, and energy-exchange. Just as our brains grow in "thinking-power" as our neurons form more and more connections and the web of neural interrelationships grows denser, so does creation grow in "creativity-power" and "life-power"— in the capacity to reveal and express the Sacred—as the web of life and energy relationships grows. There is good reason for the diversity of life and expression at all levels of creation.

The care and feeding of subtle beings is all about generating and sharing a multiplicity of "energies" and qualities through the connections they form. If new sources of information, learning, and energy become available, there will be beings who seek them out, just as in our world organisms will seek out and colonize new environments that open up to them.

It's important to appreciate that in this process, a healthy subtle organism will not engage in predation or harm another. Unless the subtle organism is sick and a pathology is involved—which can occur—subtle organisms don't "feed" on the life force of another in a parasitic manner. Rather, the exchange is a form of gifting. If I have Light to give, it benefits me as much as you if you are a willing recipient. Shakespeare's Juliet was correct when she said of love, "the more I give to thee, the more I have." On the whole, subtle beings live to offer their radiance freely to the universe and rejoice when another is benefitted by receiving what they can give. It's really no different in essence from a teacher feeling joyful and empowered by being able to share her knowledge and wisdom with her students.

People who are trained in and have experience with energy healing will be familiar with the fact that subtle energies can take different forms. There is a wide spectrum of phenomena embraced by the umbrella term "subtle energy." As a consequence, the subtle energy ecosystem is complex. This is one reason I resort to biological metaphors and descriptors; in my experience, they come the closest to conveying, however imprecisely, both the naturalness and the richness of life in the subtle worlds, as well as the fact that many of the principles that govern biological life in the physical dimension also govern "energy-based" or "spirit-based" life in the non-physical realms.

It's beyond the scope of this book to explore the different forms subtle energies can take. The important point for us in our exploration here is that subtle beings both seek sources of nourishment and nourish each other. They are all participants in and co-creators of a living universe.

FIELD NOTE 4: A LEARNING UNIVERSE

Through my life, I've observed there is a common fallacy that subtle beings are omniscient. There is an assumption that they all dwell on a "higher plane" of life where all knowledge is revealed and time and space have no mysteries. It's a reason people over the millennia have turned to the subtle worlds for guidance, advice, prophecy, and the revelation of hidden wisdom. I have known many individuals who would not make a move in their lives without consulting some subtle world guide. In the relationship of incarnate human beings to the denizens of the subtle realms, we are the learners and they are the experts.

Nothing could be further from the truth.

In this universe, we are all learners, from the vastest cosmic entity to the simplest elemental. It is a learning universe.

This is not to say that wisdom, insight, good advice, useful information, and profound perceptions cannot be found in the subtle worlds. They can. But there are equally wisdom, insight, and knowledge here in the physical realm as well. We are all experts in something, human beings no less than any other lifeform, and we all have much to learn and capacities to develop. No being on any level has a monopoly on wisdom and knowledge, or, for that matter, on good sense. Any being on any level can make a mistake; doing so can be an important part of a learning process.

A common characteristic I've experienced in nearly all the subtle beings I have encountered has been curiosity. Sometimes, if the being is non-human such as a nature spirit, this curiosity can be directed towards me; it wants to understand what makes a human tick. If the subtle being is a non-physical human, as most of my inner contacts are, then the curiosity is directed outwards towards the wondrousness of the spectrum of life throughout the universe. This spirit of inquiry arises from a desire to learn and gain information so that a consciousness can both deepen in awareness and expand in capacity, perhaps allowing new potentials to emerge. Because of this, I have observed that curiosity and desire to learn are prime motivations in life in the subtle ecosystem and especially in the formation of techno-elementals.

Within creation, life seeks out discoveries that will lead to the expansion of consciousness and beingness. Fostering learning is practically built into the functioning of the subtle realms. The paradigm is "each one teach one." Those who are more advanced, more knowledgeable, more experienced help those who are less developed. Those who have learned something new pass on their insight to those who have yet to come to it.

This arrangement is not hierarchical, though that is how we in our world often conceptualize it, with wisdom and knowledge passing down from the highest levels of spirit. As upright beings, we often project our vertical bias onto creation, seeing "up" as "good" and "down" as less so. But the subtle worlds are not like that. They operate "spherically" rather than vertically or horizontally. Every being, no matter where located on the spectrum of life or what the state of its development, has something unique and important to offer and can, in effect, be a teacher given the proper circumstances.

This is not so strange when we think about it. Though adults regularly teach children and pass on our knowledge and wisdom to those younger, there are always those times when our children can have insights we have missed (or forgotten) and can teach us something. Wisdom is not a monopoly of the eldest, as any parent who open-mindedly pays attention to her or his children can attest.

If I mention "learning," chances are many people will immediately think of "school" and the passing on of information. But learning takes many forms. My oldest son is kinesthetically-oriented; he learns best through observation and participation rather than through information gleaned from a book or a lecture. For instance, he learned to drive not in a classroom but almost entirely by observing people driving and then doing it himself. I could say that he gains information through his body as well as through his mind, or even more so.

In the subtle worlds, beings often teach and learn not through instruction but through a sharing of energy and beingness, a blending of their fields of consciousness. It would be as if, on the physical plane,

I learned dance steps by having a dancer actually move my arms and legs in the proper steps so that I had a felt sense of the muscle movements involved. More explicitly, if I want to teach a subtle being about love, I do so not by intellectually discussing love but by actually being loving, holding love in my energy field and using it to embrace that being. There is a sharing of an experience.

In the subtle realms, teaching is most often through being.

In our world, I feed my mind through learning, but I feed my body through eating. As much as I might want to live to study, I still have to nourish my body. Likewise, all the eating in the world isn't going to teach me much, except, perhaps, what causes me indigestion! But in the subtle worlds, the distinction between learning and eating isn't so direct and stark; learning can be a form of nourishment.

The bodies of subtle beings, as you might expect, are wholly different from our own. They are bodies of energy, though, like the word "frequency," this word hardly conveys the nature of the subtle substances of which these bodies are composed. It might be more accurate to think of them as bodies made up from living qualities, such as "mind-stuff" or "love-stuff." To my perception, they are often more like fields, akin perhaps to a magnetic field, than the concrete forms and shapes bodies take in the physical world. Though they may appear formless and fluid to me, sometimes little more than a swirling cloud of Light, on their native frequencies, these energy bodies are as tangible to them as our bodies are to us.

As I suggested in my story of the golden energy "blanket" I saw precipitating out from a higher realm, subtle beings exchange energy with their environment and possess a metabolism to process the energies they take in to nourish and sustain themselves. This nourishment can take two forms. It can renew and energize the substance of their unique energy field, in which case it acts analogously to food in our world. Or it can heighten, deepen, or in some way change the texture and quality of the energy in their field, expanding and evolving their capacities to be and to unfold. I think of this as a process of learning.

None of this precludes the intellectual taking in of information in a way that we would recognize as learning. But many subtle beings, while intelligent, do not have intellects or even minds as we understand them. They operate at a level of "body intelligence" or "energy intelligence" that is free from concepts but rich in direct experience. New knowledge is absorbed as an act of absorption, assimilation, and integration. You become what you learn, rather than just thinking about it or remembering it as information. In a living, learning universe, learning is a form of energy exchange that can be as nourishing and as sought after as food is for us. Understanding this will help us understand some of the characteristics of the techno-elementals.

FIELD NOTE 5: THE EIGHT FUNCTIONS

I've met many different types of subtle beings in the course of my work and explorations. While they can differ widely in terms of energy, consciousness, purpose, and so forth, as far as I can determine, they all have eight characteristics or functions in common. Understanding these functions gives us a way of understanding the nature of the techno-elementals. These eight are Identity, Organization, Exchange, Metabolism, Generativity, Connection, *Holopoiesis*, and Emergence.

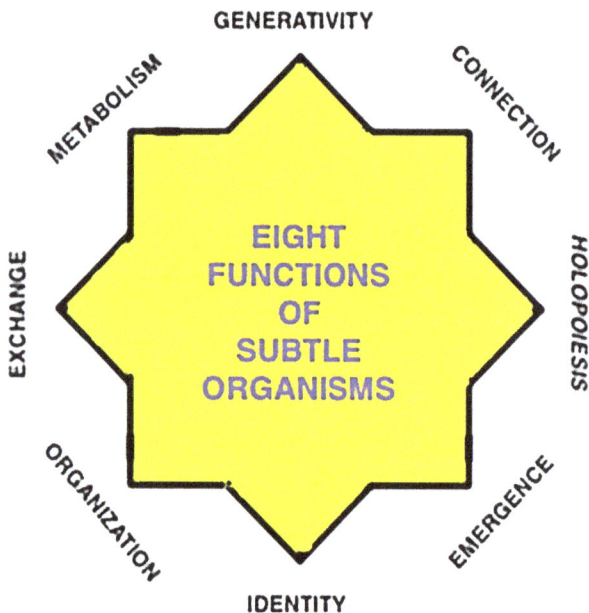

Every subtle being whom I have encountered has an **Identity**. More often than not, unless I am dealing with a human being in spirit form, this may not be anything like what we think of as "personality." It can be extremely simple, nothing more than a point of focus barely distinguishable from the sacredness that is the primal identity within all things, or it can be vastly more complex and intricate than anything you or I can manifest. Put broadly, Identity is, borrowing a term from chaos and systems theories, an "attractor" that gives coherency to the energies that constitute the subtle organism.

This identity, in my experience, does not express itself through a name. Most subtle beings I have met do not have or use names in the way we do. Instead, the distinguishing and identifying "signature" or vibration of a subtle being—who and what it is—often relates to its function, to its role in a larger, spiritual ecosystem. Or, and this is true of more advanced and complex entities, it is like a melody embedded within a symphony, the theme upon which the music plays countless variations and arrangements. Mystically, it is the Light of their being, the radiance they generate and offer to the rest of creation.

For instance, when my first mentor and partner appeared to me, I knew who he was from the totality of the vibrations emanating from him. This "signature vibration" was his name, but it was nothing I could reproduce in language. For convenience sake, I called him "John," but this was a name of my choosing, a useful designator for something wholly beyond my ability to put into words.

In my experience, I have never met a subtle being that did not have a unique identity. It might be intimately part of a collective consciousness or energy field, as are certain nature spirits and most "elementals," but in its expression, it takes on uniqueness. One reason for this is that no being acts in a vacuum apart from the rest of Creation. All beings are functioning within an environment of some nature (even if it is far beyond anything we can perceive, experience, or imagine) and in relationship to other beings and conditions. These connections and relationships are each unique, however temporary they may be, and the interacting being is shaped to some extent by this uniqueness.

Here's an example. There is a species of angels whose function is to overlight and assist human beings. Viewed from one perspective, these angels are like clones of each other, born of Light, embodying and expressing Light. But when such an angel interacts with a human being, particularly if it does so over an extended period of time as a "Guardian Angel," its energy field configures to that of the human, or humans, with whom it is aligning. Its identity is distinguishable by the nature of this relationship from that of a similar angel overlighting someone else. I think of it this way: all the angels of this type (again, borrowing from my biological training and my ecological perspective, I think of them as a "species,") are the same melody, but each angel represents a different arrangement, composed in response to the human or humans in its charge.

The second characteristic is **Organization**. This means that each subtle being possesses a coherent field of energy or spiritual substance that is organized to express its identity and its purposes within an environment. In other words, it has a "body." Because subtle beings are not constrained by material laws and necessities, such bodies may not look or behave like anything with which we are familiar in the physical world, but they are still there. Maintaining this body or energy field is an act of Holding, as I discussed in Field Note #3.

The third characteristic is **Exchange**. All subtle beings exchange energy with their environment, just as living physical beings do. However, unlike organic life, this may or may not be in order to take in nourishment. Some subtle beings *are* sustained and nourished by various life-forces circulating through the subtle worlds but others are part of enabling this circulation. For instance, I have encountered Devic beings who receive life-giving energies from higher spiritual realms, energies manifesting at too high a frequency for those on a lower dimension to perceive or receive. These beings take in these energies, process and step them down in their own beings and retransmit them in a form that those whom they are overlighting can assimilate. A metaphor might be a refinery that takes raw petroleum and refines it into a form of gasoline your car's engine can use.

The function of Exchange relates directly to the activity of Circulation I discussed earlier.

This ability to exchange energies is a function of the identity and organization of the being as a subtle organism. It also means that the subtle being has a way of processing the energy it exchanges with the environment. In effect, it has **Metabolism**, a process that provides *homeostasis*, the maintenance of the internal coherency, balance, and harmony of its personal field. This is as important to a subtle being as it is to a physical organism.

Subtle organisms, as I discussed earlier, possess **Generativity**. This means they generate and radiate subtle energies of various kinds. This generativity may be a function of the organism's metabolism or a natural outcome of its identity, but in many cases, it is a product of intent and deliberation. As I wrote in a previous Field Note, there are beings, particularly in the angelic and Devic lines of development and expression, whose function is to generate spiritual and subtle energies that bless, nourish, empower, and enlighten.

A sixth characteristic is the ability to form **Connections.** No subtle being exists wholly on its own. It needs to be able to participate in its environment, if only to express its purpose in being. It needs to form connections and relationships with the world around it.

Holopoiesis or the impulse to create wholeness is the seventh characteristic, one that arises naturally out of the formation of connections and relationships. I've already shared that, according to Dr. Lee Irwin, sentiency may be defined as the impulse to form relationship, but I would carry this one step further. Within creation is an impulse, a desire, to express the wholeness that is innate in the Sacred, the Generative Mystery that is the source of all that is. This impulse manifests as the sentiency that all life possesses, however simple that life may be. Relationships are the means, but wholeness is the goal. One characteristic, then, of the sentiency that all subtle beings—indeed all living energies in all of their forms--possess is the impulse to form and participate in wholes and thus to manifest wholeness.

As a mystic, I would call this impulse Love. Love gathers and holds creation together and acts to form relationships that can further the expression of that Love. To me, sentiency and life are about giving expression to the Love that is at the core of all things, and all subtle beings innately possess this impulse.

This does not mean that all subtle beings are automatically loving and benign. In some, this impulse has become distorted and obscured, leading to the pathology of evil. But even evil entities attempt to create wholeness; they just do so in limited, selfish, and ultimately broken ways that disrupt the larger wholeness of creation.

It also does not mean that the expression of holopoiesis and love necessarily takes a form that we incarnate humans would understand or experience as the emotion of affection and attraction we usually call love. I have encountered subtle beings who are without question loving but who are dauntingly impersonal.

Finally, the last characteristic of all the subtle beings I have met is what I call **Emergence**. I'd like another word for what I experience here, but this is the best I've come up with. In a physical organism, I would call this "change" and "growth," the capacity of life to learn, adapt, and evolve. The challenge is that subtle beings don't inhabit time and space in the way we do. The concept of evolution or change over time doesn't always fit or is an imprecise way of naming what is happening; on the other hand, in my experience, the nature of every being is to grow in the capacity to be itself and to fulfill the potential of sacredness that is the seed of life within all of us.

These eight characteristics or functions are present in one form or another in every subtle being I've met, no matter how simple or how advanced it may be. They can combine in different ways; not every subtle organism demonstrates each of these functions equally or in the same manner. But all eight are there in some form, even when it is difficult for us to see or comprehend them.

Our experience in the physical world gives us expectations for what constitutes life, form, substance, intelligence, bodies, consciousness, and so forth. The criteria we've developed serve us reasonably well in categorizing and understanding our environment. But they are inadequate once we step into the broader universe that constitutes the rest of the spectrum of life. We need to develop new ways of evaluating and describing what we are encountering in the subtle dimensions, especially as the subtle environments themselves change, sometimes drastically, when we move from one frequency or dimension of consciousness and life to another.

Over the years, acknowledging and looking for these eight functions has served me well. They represent a conceptual tool that has been helpful in gaining at least a beginning understanding of the subtle beings whom I have met or with whom I have engaged. Hopefully, they will help us here in exploring and understanding the nature of the techno-elementals.

FIELD NOTE 6: ARTISANAL FORCES

One of my most moving memories was from the summer of 1969 when I had occasion to visit Rome. One of my stops as a tourist was the Vatican where, like thousands of other visitors, I was awed by Michelangelo's paintings on the ceiling of the Sistine Chapel. But what truly struck me, moving me to tears with its beauty, was his famous sculpture of Mary holding the body of Jesus, the Pietà. It was so radiantly alive, I could hardly believe it was a piece of marble.

Michelangelo had a profound approach to his work and art as a sculptor. He saw himself less as creating something than as liberating something. Here are some quotes of his that illustrate this sentiment:

The marble not yet carved can hold the form of every thought the greatest artist has. Every block of stone has a statue inside it, and it is the task of the sculptor to discover it. The sculptor's hand can only break the spell to free the figures slumbering in the stone. I saw the angel in the marble and carved until I set him free.

If we change the words "marble" and "stone" to "life," these statements apply wonderfully well to a process of unfolding potentials—"the figures slumbering in the stone"—from the pure Potency of Being that is the Sacred by subtle beings who dedicate themselves to such an endeavor.

I learned long ago that whatever the Generative Mystery at the heart and core of creation may be, it is not definable in words nor compressible into a single image. However, one way I experience it is as pure Potency, that is, as a Presence of unconditional, universal Potential that exerts a pressure to become manifest.

Like the "marble not yet carved" that can "hold the form of every thought," this Potency holds the possibility, the potential, of everything—every atom, every molecule, every star, every planet, every blade of grass or wave or mountain, every plant, every animal, every person—that could or has or will ever exist. Whatever it is, it needs to be discovered. It needs to be freed from "slumbering in the stone."

Setting this Potency free into manifestation and expression is the work of every life in creation. In effect, God is the artisan seeking to unfold Its infinite potentials, but we—every spark of consciousness and life in creation—are the means by which it does so. We are the embodiment of this will-to-discover-and-to-become. We are each in our own way a formative force, drawing on this Potency within us to reveal its hidden Nature.

However, there are beings whose function is to work directly and deliberately with the will-to-be of the Sacred and draw forth potentials by crafting means of expression. I think of them as the artisans and architects of creation. They create the "blueprints" or "archetypal models" out of energies of thought and spirit which then eventually become clothed in matter and form to manifest in the physical realm. Thus, there is an archetypal "blueprint" for "tree," which informs the appearance of all trees of all kinds in the world.

I think of them as formative or *artisanal forces*. Who or what are these beings?

Theoretically, any being, any form of consciousness and life, could be an artisanal force, just as any person could potentially be an artist. But in fact, not everyone is an artist or has the talent and skill—or desire—to be a sculptor or painter, for example, much less one operating at the creative level of Michelangelo. Similarly, not all beings are able to tap directly into the Potency at the heart of life and bring forth new forms and patterns through which Its potential may be "set free."

When I use the term "artisanal force," I am usually thinking of those vast planetary angels and Devas (Sanskrit for "Shining One") who are the pattern-holders and overlighting intelligences for all those manifestations and functions we think of collectively as "Nature." They are, one could say, angels of form and structure.

These artisanal, formative forces might be thought of as "agents of imagination" or, to borrow Disney's wonderful descriptor, "Imagineers." In this, they are like any creative intelligence, using imagination to plunge into the heart of Potency and draw out something that will allow that Potential to take form and have expression in the world. In effect, such beings as Devas and angels are miners of life's potentials and conduits for their manifestation in the world.

The nature and function of artisanal forces is beyond the scope of this book. I bring them up because they form part of the ecosystem that defines the beings I'm calling "techno-elementals," which *are* the subject of this book.

It is one thing to imagine something; it's something else again to actually give it form. If all we have are architects, we'd never have any buildings. Other crafts, other professions, are needed to turn the ideas and possibilities in the blueprints into actual physical structures. And we also need the raw materials, the wood, stone, plaster, clay, and so on, without which no amount of artistry or craft will produce anything. I can't build a log cabin if there are no logs—or trees!

We humans tend to think in straight lines, establishing hierarchical chains of command and implementation. Thus, it's not uncommon to think of a line of creative force running from the Sacred (the inspiring Heart of Potency) through the Devic and angelic artisanal forces (architects and "Imagineers") through the diverse realms of Nature Spirits (the builders and maintenance people) to the raw materials (the "Elementals"), those that ultimately Hold the pattern and energy field in substance, structure, and form. Remember that everything is alive, so the bricks and mortar that go into the structure of a building are as much an expression of creative life as the architects that imagined the form of the building and drew up the blueprints.

My oldest daughter, Kaitlin, is the lead animator for a video game company. She performs or oversees a number of tasks necessary to give visual expression to the narrative ideas of the game designers, but one she has been concentrating on lately is motion capture or "mo-cap." A modern video game is often a complex production in which key elements of the story are presented to the player in "cut scenes," or small movies. To create them, actors play out the scene from the game while wearing suits that enable their every movement to be wirelessly transmitted into a computer where it is rendered into a three-dimensional representation or picture. This representation is then "skinned" or given the outer appearance needed by the story of the game by the animators. Thus, the actors may be turned into elves confronting orcs or a human space explorer meeting aliens. A familiar example of this process is the way the actor Andy Serkis is transformed on the screen into Gollum in the Lord of the Rings and Hobbit movies and Supreme Leader Snoke in *Star Wars: The Force Awakens*.

Here is a process by which an idea existing purely in the imagination of a writer and game designer is translated into physical, three-dimensional action by actors which is then further translated into digital images in a computer screen with which a player can interact. There is a transition of energy and intent through three different realms of existence, and there are a variety of individuals, functions, and processes making this transition possible: designers, writers, actors, directors, programmers, artists, and animators, to name some. There is an ecosystem of creative manifestation and artisanal energy interacting and collaborating to "free the image from the stone."

The same is true in the cosmos as divine ideas are translated into different realms of expression and energy.

It's tempting to see this as a one-way, hierarchical process, from idea to execution and expression, and from one perspective it is. But in my experience in contacting a variety of these beings over the years, it gives an incomplete and thus distorted picture of what is happening. We need to perceive holistically and ecologically and to think of the whole system, not just parts of it.

In this case, it's helpful to think of a "formative process" or a "formative system," one in which "artisans," "builders," and "raw materials" are all partners and equally integral to the whole system. We separate them out for convenience and because it's true that certain beings specialize in certain capacities and functions, but they all participate in a single enterprise whose object is to give expression to the potentials held "sleeping" within the Presence of the Sacred.

Actually, it's not such a stretch to think systemically. I've had friends who are architects, and before they begin to draft a final blueprint of a building, they are informed by the nature of the materials with which they will be working. Things are possible with steel that may not be possible with wood or brick, and vice versa. They have to know the capacities of the structural components from which the building is assembled. Not incorporating that information—that attunement to the physical materials involved—means their imagination cannot be grounded in physical reality or worse, that what they build collapses because materials were used in the wrong way.

It works the other way as well. Whatever potentials lie in stone, clay, wood, and other materials that could be expressed in novel ways will remain undiscovered without the energy of imagination and intention held by the architects and builders. Without the sculptor, the angel remains imprisoned and unseen within the marble. The marble doesn't become what it could become.

There is something else we need to understand about the artisanal, formative forces. In our world, we often associate creativity with imagination and thought; that is, it is a mental exercise, though fueled by passion and artistic sensitivity.

In the subtle worlds, however, particularly in those spiritual realms where the planetary Devas and angels function, it is Life that draws out Life. It is not so much thought as we understand it, though certainly intelligence and skill are involved, but rather Love and Joy as sacred, creative qualities that are the "mining instruments." We might think of an artisanal presence like a Deva willing some new form into being, but it is more as if it is evoking it through the focused power of its own life, its own joy, its own love. Intention is certainly there, but it is not intention or will acting on its own, exerting a dominance over the substances of creation. It is more like a reaching into the Sacred Potency to call forth the intent to be that is potential within the form that is being drawn forth. As I say, life calls to life, inviting it to take up or take on a new form, a new way of being, a new way of expressing the infinite potential within the Sacred. It is a collaboration.

Certainly, this is true in my daughter's work. The actors give feedback to Kaitlin as a director that helps improve the script. Playtesters, ordinary people brought into the studio at different stages in the creative process to try out the game provide information on what is working and what isn't. It's not a one-way flow from producer to consumer.

And just as a human creator, such as an artist or an architect, can feel an aliveness, a joy, a surge of energy in the act of creating and seeing what has come forth, so the artisanal force generates energy and a heightening of life and beingness.

There have been times in my interactions with the subtle worlds when I've been invited to merge with the life and consciousness of a Devic being acting as an artisanal force. I have no illusions that what I experienced was anything near the whole of that Deva's presence and activity, only as much of it as I could perceive, hold and assimilate. I have a sense of being protected during such engagements lest I become overwhelmed and harmed by the intensity of what was happening. But I could see enough, experience enough, to know that a fierce and radiant love and joy and an almost unbearable exuberance and ecstasy of life lay at the heart of a being like this and what it does to bring new forms, new possibilities, new ideas into the world. I think of these beings as the lovers of God; more than just artisans, they open the gates of life by being in love with life and with the Sacred Presence that is its source. They are the Beloveds of the Potency at the heart of all things.

FIELD NOTE 7: ELEMENTALS

In the Western esoteric and alchemical traditions, the world was thought to be formed from four basic elements: earth, air, fire, and water. Each of these elements not only had physical characteristics but spiritual and esoteric qualities as well. Embodying these qualities were beings called "elementals." Thus, there were elementals of fire, elementals of water, and so on.

Elements and the elementals were considered the living building blocks out of which the world was formed. In modern times, we have other ways of describing the building blocks of the universe. We talk about atoms, sub-atomic particles, and quantum level phenomena. Gravity, electromagnetism, and the strong and weak nuclear forces are the four fundamental forces that we now know. The elementals of our ancestors are just a fantasy, relegated to myth and superstition.

But are they?

Science has given us much valuable information about the structure of the physical universe and how it works. What it hasn't done yet is give us the same insights about the non-physical or subtle side of the world and the cosmos. While elementals may play no role in the theories of modern physics, they play a key role in the life of the subtle realms. Existing as part of the subtle environment that surrounds us, they are an integral part of the creative process by which things come into being. They are often among the most powerful of all subtle beings.

In my first Field Note, I described a process of attuning to different frequencies of life within my sofa. I'm going to use a similar process to explore the nature of elementals. In this case, I'm going to begin with a small stone that I have sitting on my desk. There's nothing overtly special about it as stones go. It's just an ordinary garden-variety stone that, in fact, I picked up from my garden.

There is a story behind it, though. Several years ago, I took a trip to visit Findhorn, the international spiritual community where, in the early Seventies, I had been a co-director. I decided I wanted to take a stone with me that would be an energetic link to my home. I looked around my yard for a stone small enough to carry easily in my pocket and found several candidates.

I asked each stone I picked up if it would like to come with me. It was the energetically proper thing to do, an act of respect and courtesy to the life within the stone. Each time I did so, the response was no. Whatever the energy linkages were that the particular stone had with the local subtle (and physical) environment, it didn't want them broken. I had about given up when I spied this particular small, roundish stone lying near the path leading up to our front door. Something about it caught my attention, and when I picked it up and explained what I wanted, it responded with a burst of energy that I took to be an enthusiastic yes.

For accuracy's sake, I must say that although the focal point of this "communication" or energetic impulse that said "no" or "yes" was the particular stone involved—and it certainly seemed to me I was in touch with a specific entity or intelligence—it could also have been the "voice" of the local environment making itself known, a resistance or a willingness within the whole web of energetic relationships to be changed by my actions. For convenience sake, I write of experiences like this as if I were having a conversation with a person, but of course, in instances like this, this isn't true. There are clear and meaningful energy exchanges which carry information, but in many cases, precisely what is "speaking" to me isn't that clear and certainly not that anthromorphic.

Whatever the source of the "yes," this little stone became a constant companion with me. When I stopped traveling, I "retired" it to my desk where it has seemed content to be.

As a consequence of the relationship between us, there is an energetic field around this stone that resonates to me. At this level, the living energy of the stone is impressed and shaped by my own energy. I have no doubt that a person capable of psychometry, the ability to psychically read the energy fields around physical objects, would pick up on the connection this stone has with me and would be able to glean some information from it about me.

Had I put the stone back in my yard when I was done with it, this relational level would over time have returned to the state it had been in when I first picked it up. At that time, the energy field around it was impressed, shaped and defined by the energies of the soil, the plants, the weather, and so forth that made up its subtle and physical environment. Eventually, the traces of its connection to me would likely disappear, though this would depend on how deeply and deliberately I had impressed my energy on the stone in the first place. A friend of mine who has worked as a psychometrist on archeological expeditions in South America and the Middle East has been able to read information energetically impressed upon pottery shards and other materials left by individuals who died thousands of years ago. In the subtle realms, time doesn't always count for much.

Beyond this relational field, I come to the identity of the stone itself, its "self" or beingness as a stone. It's at this level that I come into contact with what I think of as an elemental energy. It's the elemental or foundational identity of this particular stone, a living, intelligent force that's holding it in existence as a stone, shaping its molecules and atoms to be a stone and not something else.

I think of this frequency of energy, life and consciousness as the spirit of my stone, it's unique identity. There is, however, a deeper level. Here I am in touch not with a stone but with Stone, the Intelligence and Life of stone itself, present wherever stone or minerals are found on earth and perhaps in the universe itself.

This is what I think of as a planetary or even a cosmic Elemental, one of the fundamental artisans of the world, bringing into form creative ideas born at the beginning of creation.

What is both wondrous and paradoxical is that both the elemental spirit of my stone and the cosmic Elemental of Stone are essentially the same presence, the same life. The particular is an expression of the universal and the universal is found in the life and specificity of the particular.

A close friend of mine is Dorothy Maclean, one of the three founders of the Findhorn Foundation community in Northern Scotland. Her contact with the Devas was what initially led to the creation of

Findhorn's world-famous garden. She told me of an experience she had had in which she had been attracted to a pebble she saw on a beach. She thought she'd tune into it, expecting to contact a simple, even primitive form of life and consciousness. After all, what else would one expect from a pebble?

To her amazement, she found herself in contact with a vast, cosmic Intelligence, one whose presence seemed to extend endlessly out into the universe. These were its beginning words to her:

> Yes, I whom you have contacted am concerned with vastly more than your planet, for I contain or am connected with mineral life which exists in various stages throughout creation. Nature is full of paradox, in that, as you seek contact with what you consider a lower form of life, you in fact contact a more universal being. The human mind codifies and formulates, which is within its right and purpose, but forgets that all is one, that God is in all, and that the basic substance of life, which seems most devoid of sensitive consciousness, is held in its state of existence by its opposite, a vast consciousness, too vast for you to do more than sense its fringes and know that I extend beyond your imagination as yet.

She called this Being the "Cosmic Angel of Stone." If you are interested, you can read the full account of her experience and the entire message this Being had to offer in her book *To Hear the Angels Sing*.

I want to give another example.

In my backyard, I have a maple tree. This tree has been an integral part of our family's life ever since we moved into our house over thirty years ago. Its leaves have shaded our back porch from the summer sun when it was hot. Its trunk and branches supported a tree house in which our kids played for years, and one large branch held a swing.

When I attune to this maple tree, I'm aware of an intelligence and a spirit. Unlike my little stone, it is an active, self-aware, and generative presence, though not in the same way that I am as a human. When I attune to it, I feel myself in the presence of a being who can form a relationship with me but whose life and consciousness is independent and cannot be shaped by me. There is an individual spirit here that is actively engaged with its subtle and physical environment in ways that don't involve me. Indeed, as with any loving relationship, it can influence me energetically as much as I influence it.

If I turn my attention and attunement to a frequency that is more "fundamental" or "deeper" than that at which I encounter its individual spirit, I discover what I would call the "elemental spirit of the maple tree." At this level, my individual tree is part of a larger collective field of being in which all maple trees anywhere in the world participate. This is like saying that all human beings share the same human genome even though it expresses uniquely in each of us.

Going deeper, though, I encounter a level of energy and identity that is even more fundamental than that of "maple tree." This is the identity of being a tree, an elemental archetype shared by all trees everywhere.

But it doesn't end there, for the expression of "tree-ness" is itself a manifestation of a more elemental identity, that of being a plant. Here I mentally touch the Elemental of Plant, also one of the fundamental spiritual and energetic artisans of our world.

What exactly am I touching into here? In effect, I'm moving through layers of identity from the particular to the universal, from a state that is more focused to one that is vast and complex. It is at one and the same time the same Being and yet, as it differentiates itself into an infinite number of specific manifestations, it becomes many specific beings. In effect, there seems to me to be the foundational "Elementals of Substance" and the particularized "Elementals of Manifestation and Form."

In both cases, the one characteristic that stands out, at least to my perception and awareness, is a dedication to the function of Identity (one of the eight I described in Field Note #5). This function of Identity manifests the quality I call "Holding," that which provides stability and preserves or holds a particular structure.

This, to me, defines the nature of the form and function of Elementals. They are the Holders. They maintain the essential nature and identity of something so that around that core, multiple variations and manifestations can take place. Using a musical metaphor, we might think of Elementals as providing the basic rhythm on which a melody and all its arrangements can be based.

One of my subtle colleagues once said to me, "Think of elementals as the finger that holds down the knot so that the bow of a specific creation might be formed and tied."

FIELD NOTE 8: NATURE SPIRITS

I live in a valley surrounded on three sides by foothills of the Cascade Mountain Range in western Washington State.

Running through most of the length of this valley is a long lake, Lake Sammamish, which is about a five-minute walk from my house. If I turn my attention to it, I can sense the subtle energy of this lake as I go about my business at home. If I walk down to the lake, though, I can attune to the elementals of water that are there. Their focus is purely on "being water." As with my little stone, if I go to a deeper frequency of these elementals, I discover a single Presence, a planetary Elemental of water.

However, this is not the only Presence I can contact in the lake. There is another who appears to me as a feminine being, though not a human one. She is energetically very powerful, her field of awareness and life embracing and exchanging subtle energies with the nearby hills and mountains, including all the humans that live along her shoreline. She is the Deva or angel of the lake and as such, she is deeply attuned to water and its qualities. I think of her as the Lady of the Lake.

What she is not is an elemental of water. She is what I would call a "nature spirit," not an elemental. The configuration of her energy field, its "tone" and "composition" is different from that of the elemental beings.

Looking back at our eight functions, if elementals basically support the function of Identity, nature spirits are those who facilitate the functions of connection and energy exchange between individual beings and their environments. They are those who enable the process of circulation and absorption. Metaphorically, elementals are "solids" while nature spirits are "fluids," an oversimplification based on physical imagery but perhaps helpful in showing the distinction between them.

The difference between an elemental and a nature spirit lies largely in function and on which of the eight functions of subtle life is emphasized more than the others. In my experience, nature spirits deal largely with the circulation and exchange of subtle energies between the organisms they are overlighting and the subtle environment in which those organisms exist, as well as assisting as best they can the health and evolution of those organisms. If elementals serve a will-to-be, the nature spirits serve a will-to-unfold-and-develop.

Is an elemental more powerful than a nature spirit, or vice versa? No. They cannot be compared in that way. The artisanal forces conceive the shape of the bow, the nature spirits provide, fold and shape the ribbons, and the elementals hold the knot that keeps the bow from disintegrating. All are necessary to the bow, none more powerful or needed than the other. Each has its role.

Think for a moment of writing. I have thoughts I want to put into words. The alphabet provides the elemental forms necessary for me to do this. The letters are the elementals from which words are formed. Language, in this case English, sets up the rules and interactions—the grammar and syntax—for connecting these words, establishing relationships between them that allow meaning to emerge; this is comparable to the nature spirits. The imagination and thinking that determines the thoughts to which the letters, words, and grammar will give form, releasing from them from the potentials of my mind, are the artisanal forces. Together, the system they all form is the Artisanal Force that produces the content on this page. They are all equally important to convey my thoughts to you.

Terms like "nature spirits" and "elementals," like many words referring to subtle phenomena, are not always used with accuracy or precision in our culture (assuming they are used at all!). We do not as a culture have the familiarity, the experience, or the concepts to deal with what for so many is simply fantasy or superstition, or even if real, something to be left alone while we get on with "real life."

Even if we did give these phenomena the attention that they deserve, the plasticity and fluidity of the subtle worlds means it is not always easy to discern the energetic boundaries and differences between one species or class of subtle organism and another. I've been aware of subtle beings of one kind or another for over seventy years, and I still can find it challenging to know what I'm encountering. Often, it may not matter. Here's an experience that illustrates this:

I had gone into the kitchen to get a drink of water. I filled a glass with water from the tap, and as I was lifting it up to drink, there suddenly appeared in the water in the glass a small being that identified itself as a water spirit. It spoke with great urgency and passion and said, in effect, "When you use water, please send loving, healing, and uplifting energy to water everywhere and to the kingdom of the water spirits. Many of our kind are suffering and are under siege from the continuing and increasing pollution of water by humanity. We need energetic support and blessing from which we can draw strength."

This was a heartfelt appeal, and I had an image of water spirits in rivers and in the ocean trying to cope with the disruption of their environment by all the ways we are polluting the water. I felt a concern on the part of this little being that there could come a time when pure or drinkable water would be a rarity, and all life would suffer.

Tuning into this being, I had a sense that many water spirits were weakening under the onslaught of the toxicity that human beings dump into their realm--not that they are poisoned themselves but that their contact with the water is weakened and they are driven back, so to speak, unable to make full connection with the water they serve.

This being's request seemed to suggest that if we each sent love and Light and gratitude to the spirits of water, that they could draw on those energies to renew their ability to keep the etheric and energetic qualities of water clean and strong.

I'd never had an experience quite like this. Was this a water nature spirit or a water elemental? Frankly, I don't know, though I suspect it was the former. It was certainly identified with the element of water, but it was a being whose intent was to serve that element wherever it might be found, which felt to me more like the consciousness and energy of a water-oriented nature spirit. The important thing is that it didn't matter. It was the message that was important, not the messenger. The appeal of this being, whatever kind of water spirit it was, was so heartfelt that now whenever I pour myself a glass of water or take a shower or bath, I remember to offer my Light and blessing and love to water everywhere.

The distinction between an elemental and a nature spirit can become even less clear when we leave the realm of nature and enter the realm of human artifacts and our human-created, built environment. It's here that we find the different types of beings that collectively I refer to as techno-elementals, the subject of this book. To understand them, we need to first look at the energetic anatomy of our artifacts, for these provide the specialized environment in which these beings live and function.

FIELD NOTE 9: THE ANATOMY OF AN ARTIFACT

When I look at myself in the mirror, I see "me," David Spangler. But, leaving psychology and the idea of multiple personalities out of consideration here, how many "me's" could I see?

I could see the "Human Genome Me," my hominid form and features evolved over millions of years. I share this "me" with every other human being on earth; we all have the same basic genetic foundation.

Then I could see the "Personal Genetic Me." This is the specific body I've inherited from my parents, the unique way in which the elements of the human genome are configured in my personal case. This is my "DNA identity." It distinguishes me from every other human being on earth.

Third, I could see the "Personality Me," or the "Everyday Me." This is who I think I am—and who I present to others—based on years of experience, on my intentions, choices, desires, dreams, and so on. This "me" is generally who is meant when people talk about "David Spangler."

I could go on to talk about "subtle me's" and "spiritual me's," but this would take us too far afield. However, there is another "me" that is there before me in the mirror, and that is me as environment.

My body is an environmental niche in which trillions of microbial organisms that are "not-me" live and evolve. These organisms don't know anything about me as a person or about my Identity, my plans, my hopes, my dreams, or my fears. They do not share my DNA nor my human genome. I am simply a place to live and a place to find food. Some of these organisms are beneficial, even essential, to my health. Some are opportunistic, invading my body and, in their growth and proliferation, causing me pain and disease. Some are simply neutral, neither harming me nor helping me but using my body as a home.

Whether I see myself when I look in the mirror at my body or I see an environment colonized by myriad, diverse other organisms, depends entirely on my perspective, that is, on how I am looking. One is a macro-view—the body as a whole—and the other is a microscopic view—the body as a living petri dish.

Depending on my purpose, I can pay attention to any one of these four "me's," each of which has its role to play. If I want to understand human evolution and species development, as well as gaining insights into what makes humanity the way it is, I will look to the human genome for understanding. If I want to understand tendencies in my personal life, potentials as well as weaknesses I may have, I will look to my personal DNA. If I want to shape my life through my thinking and feeling, my intention and imagination, I will work with my psyche and personality. And if I want to deal with infections on the one hand or strengthen my digestion on the other, I will look at ways of making the internal biochemical environment of my body either inimical or hospitable to the appropriate bacteria.

Our artifacts are similar. If I look at my coffee cup, I can see it simply as a cup, handy for that morning dose of caffeine. Or I can see it as a compilation of overlapping frequencies and fields of energy, each of which potentially acts as an environment or a touch point for a subtle being. From one perspective, it is a thing; from the other, energetically, like my body, it is a miniature universe.

Let me illustrate this with a couple of items sitting on my desk. The first is a hand-carved, reddish-brown chalice, six inches in height, carved from the wood of an apple tree. The bowl and rim are not round but an interestingly irregular oval that when I look at it reminds me of the curving canyons of the American Southwest where I lived as a teenager.

When I attune to this chalice with love and appreciation, I'm aware of a range of frequencies to which I can attune, just like the different "me's" in the mirror.

The equivalent to the human genome is what I experience as a long, deep wave of energy and life which, when I attune to it, brings into my awareness primal elementals of substance, like "Wood," "Tree,"

"Plant." These elemental presences seem to me like the mountains I can see on the horizon where I live: distant and immense. Just as I could get in my car and drive to the mountains, I could expend energy to make contact with these elemental forces, if there were a need to do so. But these Beings are timeless, vast, and far beyond the range of normal human consciousness. I might as well try to have a conversation with one of the mountains. I do, though, draw a deep sense of stability from their presence and a sense of attunement to Gaia, the life of the planet as a whole.

Universal principles and presences become specific manifestations in the world. "Plant" differentiates into millions of species of vegetation. "Tree" manifests as the many types of trees that populate the land, including apple trees, of which there are over 7500 known varieties. But my chalice was carved from one specific tree and is in itself a specific expression of apple wood. As such, it has a unique energy field.

Like the "Goldilocks Level" I described in my sofa in the first Field Note, this energy field is sentient and alive. It is formed from the energy of the apple wood but it is shaped by the application of human energies in the form of thought, imagination, the love and care that went into its crafting, and the energy from the body of the artist who made this chalice. It is no longer "pure" apple wood energy but a hybrid born of human interaction and intent. The apple wood is still there and it would be possible to evoke from it an apple wood nature spirit. However, in its normal "resting" or "native" state, without such an evocation, the energy field of the chalice is a manifestation of human imagination and purpose blended with the characteristics of a natural substance.

In the case of this chalice, this field is particularly alive precisely because this object is hand-made. A person poured his love, his skill, his craftsmanship, his artistry, his vision, his care into the carving of this chalice. He energized it with his life. The chalice is not simply the product of human design; it is a product of active, mindful partnership with the spirit and substance of the apple wood. This creates a more active and vibrant field of subtle life around the chalice than there is, say, around my mass-produced water glass, or around my sofa, which was also manufactured in a factory rather than crafted in an artist's studio.

The individual "Goldilocks Field" of life around this chalice—this living "chalice spirit"— holds and maintains its energetic coherency and identity as an artifact. It is roughly equivalent to my unique DNA. What is important to realize when it comes to our artifacts is that this "personal level" of energy, like my body's DNA, is shaped from two sources, two "parents," if you will. The nature elemental, whatever it may be, is one source (and in the case of this chalice, it is that of wood and specifically of apple wood), while human intention and energy is the other. The apple tree is not going to produce a chalice on its own. It has no will or capacity to do so. Apples, yes; chalices, no. It has taken a human being to bring this chalice-expression of apple wood into being. This blending of two distinct energy sources gives this artifact a unique hybrid energy field. It is the product of human imagination, thought, feeling, and will interacting with nature. It is a co-creation. As such, it brings into being a new subtle environment which is not found in nature on its own and which can attract subtle organisms seeking to benefit or learn from it.

All subtle fields, whether they surround a person or an artifact, have two basic functions. The first is to hold the energetic structure of purpose or identity. For example, my own subtle energy field holds my identity as a living energy pattern incarnating in the physical world. The second is to provide connection with the vast realm of subtle forces and energies, many of which provide needed nourishment and blessing.

These two basic functions may manifest in very simple ways, without much complexity. If sentiency is the capacity to form relationships and thereby to promote wholeness, then the sentiency is low. However, the more energy of intent and life that is poured into an artifact, either in its creation or in its use, the more active and sentient this field becomes and the more influence it exerts energetically.

This influence is characterized by its hybrid nature and, in my experience, is not the same as what emanates from a natural object.

Thus, my chalice, though made of wood, radiates a different kind of energy—a different "flavor"—than does my maple tree.

It is this difference that marks the emergence of what I think of as a techno-elemental. If it becomes stimulated and heightened enough, usually by the presence of human subtle energies and thought directed towards it, this hybrid field can particularize even more, becoming more active, more sentient, more responsive. Metaphorically, it becomes the "personality" of the artifact, a distinct, individual field of being that can change and evolve through interaction with human beings. Depending on its nature, its own complexity and skill, it may or may not take on a specific form detached from the artifact itself.

This is particularly likely to happen if the artifact, by virtue of what it is, is connected to a larger field of energy. For instance, in the case of my chalice, it is connected to the archetype of the Grail, a powerful source of energy indeed. The chalice is a cup for drinking, but in Western mythology and religious tradition, it is also the symbol of the Holy Grail, the cup that held the blood of Christ. As such, it becomes a container that can hold the presence of the Sacred. The Grail is thus a symbol of healing, blessing, and the restoration of wholeness to anything that has been broken.

My wooden chalice is not meant to hold liquid or be used for drinking. It is an artifact meant for an altar as a symbol of Light and sacredness. Its purpose is to create connections between a person and the deep, healing, inspiring mysteries of Life. It resonates to the archetype of the Holy Grail and all that that means. I know all this was in the mind of the person who made this chalice for me. It was there in his artistic intent and thus was a resonance built into this artifact.

I also treat this chalice as a point of connection to the Grail and all that it symbolizes. For me, the Grail is a symbol of incarnation, yours and mine, and of the power of a human being to hold and embody sacredness, becoming a source of blessing and wholeness in the world. In the Incarnational Spirituality that I teach, we are each Grails.

For this reason, this chalice resonates through the intents of both its creator and its user, me, with larger, more powerful energy fields.

Consequently, when I tune into its unique life-field, I am sometimes greeted by a small being that looks to me like a living flame, one that holds the "essence" or "archetype" of "chalice-ness." I mean by this I can feel within it the potential of all chalices to be containers of holiness. This presence emerges from the connection this artifact has with the "Grail Field."

The ability to create objects that connect so directly to archetypal and sacred sources of energy and blessing is part of our innate capacity as human beings to manifest artisanal forces. This is more than an artistic ability. It is a transpersonal force that can bring spiritual realities and qualities into expression in the physical world. It releases an artisanal energy that in this instance transcends both the artist who carved the chalice and myself as the one who interacts with it.

In the case of this chalice, the techno-elemental that is the hybrid spirit of its energetic life is capable because of the resonances to which it has been exposed of linking to this sacred, artisanal force, making it a living part of this artifact. It can, in other words, touch into and give expression to some aspect of the soul of humanity. Not all artifacts have this capacity.

In this, the chalice acts as a kind of talisman, that is, an artifact that has been imbued with an ability to reach beyond its form and function, giving its "personality" level of energy a link to something transcendent, some presence or focus of energy existing in an archetypal or spiritual level of existence.

To sum up, when I attune to it, my chalice has a foundational level that resonates to an elemental of substance and a field of identity and purpose that is unique to it and that is the foundation of its techno-elemental expression. It also manifests a more complex energy structure of sentiency and presence that is linked with transpersonal fields of spirit and presence.

Now let me examine the "artifactual subtle anatomy" of another object, one that I'm sure will be familiar to you.

This is a plastic sculpture of Yoda, the Jedi Master from George Lucas's *Star Wars* films. This iconic figure sits on my desk and stares at me while I work.

Here, upon clairvoyant investigation, are layers or frequencies of energy similar to those I perceive with my chalice, but their expression is very different. There are the deep elementals of substance, in this case, a mix of organic materials. As far as I can tell, there is no Deva or Elemental of Plastic as such; it is itself an artifact of our technology.

There is also a "Goldilocks Field" of living, sentient energy—the field of purpose and identity—but it is undifferentiated, again as far as I can determine. There is no "spirit of Yoda sculpture" the way there is a spirit of the chalice. The living field around the chalice knows it is a chalice. The plastic that makes up Yoda knows it's plastic but doesn't know it's a figure of Yoda—or a figure of anything, for that matter.

Largely, this is because this is not a hand-crafted object but one manufactured, presumably by the thousands (there are a lot of *Star Wars* Yoda fans!) in a factory by programmed machines.

However, there is still an energy of human intent and design. It still possesses a hybrid energy field. After all, someone thought up Yoda in the first place and created the first Yoda figure, the puppet used in the movies. Likewise, some artist made the mold for this sculpture, perhaps as a computer file. Plastic, much less dead, organic plant and animal matter from millions of years ago, did not just arrange itself spontaneously to look like Yoda. One doesn't drill oil wells and find little statues of Yoda coming up from the earth along with the petroleum from which plastic is synthesized. So, human imagination, thought, and design was involved in creating my little Yoda. But unlike my chalice, where the human presence was in direct one-to-one touch with the apple wood, here the human presence is distant in time and space and masked by the automated manufacturing process. The *idea* of Yoda exists in the mind of humans, but the plastic that forms the *body* of Yoda is touched and molded by machines.

I found this statue of Yoda in a store. When I bought it and brought it home, it was energetically just a neutral artifact, alive in the sense that all things are alive, but not particularly differentiated. It had the unique shape of Yoda on the outside, but its energy field could have belonged to a block of plastic or a stone.

However, Yoda is an iconic figure for me. He represents the

archetype of the wise and powerful elder in touch with the deep mysteries and forces of the universe. He is the shaman, the medicine man, the adept, the teacher, the initiator. He is a master of the Force that unites all life and binds the cosmos together. For me, as for many others, he is a rich and powerful imaginal figure. (Years ago, I met a Zen abbot who was the head teacher or *roshi* of his monastery. He met me wearing a T-shirt emblazoned with the figure of Yoda. This was not what I had expected to see him wearing, so he grinned and patted his chest. "My lineage," he said, which immediately endeared him to me. "Mine, too," I replied!)

To me, the figure of Yoda *means* something. It is an icon, a portal, into something ineffable. I have projected that meaning onto this little statue, energizing it with my love and appreciation. As a consequence, the living field of this artifact is no longer neutral. It resonates to the archetype of wisdom and connection that Yoda represents to me. It also resonates to the field of imagination that Yoda occupies within the minds and hearts of *Star Wars* fans because I share that collective imagination.

Do I see a small "Yoda being" attached to this statue the way I see a "Grail being" attached to my chalice? No. The idea of Yoda, though widespread, doesn't have the deep roots in human consciousness as does that of the cup, chalice, or Grail, an archetypal container that has been part of human civilization for thousands of years and one that has figured in many rituals in many cultures. Its living field reflects and is shaped by my own Yoda projections and meanings, that is, how the idea of Yoda lives in me, not how it might live independently in this statue.

If a human artist created a Yoda figure by hand and invested it through his or her love and artistic thought and design with all the resonances to the archetypal Wise Old Man, then it would be different. Then the living field of such a Yoda would likely manifest a "Yoda spirit." But as it stands, no such dedicated intention went into its manufacture in the factory.

Still, its field of identity and purpose is an environment resonating to an energy of human intention, and as such, it can attract other kinds of subtle beings who find that environment nourishing and who might use it as a temporary link with my human world. If a Yoda-shaped being did appear to me, it most likely would not be something generated by the statue itself but a "Rider," something like the equivalent of a microbial organism living in the microbiome of my digestive system.

I have not "talismanized" the statue of Yoda, so it is not by itself connected to transpersonal, transcendent, or spiritual energies. When I see Yoda sitting on my desk, I can in the moment feel connected to such energies myself, but that is a different thing, one in which an imaginative image is an inspirational catalyst for contact with higher energies. My statue can act as such an image, but, unlike my chalice, it is not a conduit for those energies in itself.

These two examples I have used to illustrate the kind of subtle energy fields that can exist around our artifacts are different from each other. One is a hand-crafted wooden chalice and the other is a mass-produced plastic statue. However, there are three things they have in common. The first is that, as I discussed in Field Note #1, both are extensions of the energy field of human consciousness and thought. Both give access to the realm of human imagination. One resonates with all the thoughts and feelings around cups, grails, chalices, and their mythic and spiritual meanings in human evolution. Holding my chalice, for instance, I can find myself in touch with the whole imaginal world of King Arthur and the quest for the Holy Grail, a powerful image in the Western mystical and esoteric traditions. On the other hand, my statue of Yoda resonates with the stories of Star Wars and the Force, which have become engraved in the popular imagination, and beyond them, to their roots in the heroic narrative—the Hero's Journey described by mythologist Joseph Campbell—that is so much a part of Western culture. In other words, if I choose to attune to this level, each of these artifacts is connected to a "cloud" of related images and thought-forms existing within the collective imagination and thinking of humanity. This cloud, in turn, can resonate to the artisanal, creative forces that are part of humanity's spiritual heritage and power—and, in the case of my chalice, it does so resonate.

This "cloud" of human energy and thought, intention, and

imagination creates an energetic environment that is attractive to subtle beings who wish to learn from and be nourished by our quality of beingness. Just as we may study the art of an ancient culture to discover what the people of that culture may have been like, so subtle beings can align with the energy fields of our artifacts as a way of understanding who we are, what we are like, and the spiritual mysteries and forces enfolded in our incarnational process. This is potentially as true for my Yoda—or any of the other iconic action figures that I have arrayed along my desk—as it is for my chalice or for any other artifact in my house, including the house itself. I shall have more to say about these subtle beings, whom I think of as "Riders," in the next Field Note.

There is another field of energy that can be found around our artifacts. As I discussed in Field Note #1, it is an aura of psychic connection, the "Velcro field" that can pick up and hold stray subtle energies moving through the environment. How active (or "sticky") this field is depends on a number of factors, including the substance from which the object is made, its use within the human world, and so on. People sit on my sofa in the living room all the time, for instance, and it is more involved in the activity of people coming and going. Yoda, on the other hand, is tucked away on my desk where I can see him but the statue is relatively removed from the flow of energy moving through the house; also, I'm pretty much the only one who handles it, and even then, I don't do so very often. Potentially, it's not as much of a "psychic lint collector" as my sofa.

My chalice and my Yoda are two simple objects. The subtle energy environments that surround things such as machinery or buildings, not to mention computers, are more complex. The basic principle, though, is the same. What we create lives in its way in the subtle realms and forms opportunities for relationships and connections that offer new possibilities for nourishment, learning, and evolution. We create, both physically and energetically, environments that otherwise would not exist, environments of the techno-elementals.

FIELD NOTE 10: TECHNO-ELEMENTALS

Techno-elementals is a word I coined to describe those subtle beings who either establish contact and associate with humanity through our artifacts or as a consequence of our technology. It's not a precise term by any means as it includes both the hybridized elemental beings I described in a previous Field Note. It can also include subtle beings who seek to perform within the human domain a service of circulation and exchange akin to that offered by nature spirits, as well as beings who are simply curious and interested in humanity and who use the things we produce and build as a point of contact and linkage. I suppose a more precise term would be "techno-subtles," but techno-elementals feels better rolling off the tongue! It captures, I believe, in an alliterative way the sense of what I want to convey.

To help me differentiate as much as possible between the different types of techno-elementals I have observed over the years, I think of them in four categories. First, there are the particular manifestations of subtle life connected directly with the artifact, whatever it may be, however simple or complex it may be. If "elementals" refers to subtle beings found in nature, I play on this word and refer to this category as the "**Artifactals**." Second, there are the "**Riders**," beings who are attracted to the energy field of the artifact as an environment either to provide service or to gain learning and nourishment. Third, there are the "**Allies**," beings who connect with the energy fields of our artifacts and technology in order to help us. Finally, there are those I call the "**Sacramentals**," beings of Light and blessing deliberately invoked and aligned with an object that then serves as a talisman, a point of contact with their qualities and energies.

Before discussing these in detail, I want to emphasize that when dealing with subtle phenomena, boundaries are not necessarily hard and fast. I use these four categories for convenience to help me understand just what I might be sensing and how to deal with it, but there is nothing rigid about them. For instance, the dividing line between "Allies" and "Sacramentals" is particularly permeable, with a being acting as both or as one or the other depending on the circumstances. It is the same with "Riders;" one of these might be a being who is only temporarily present in the field of an artifact or it might be one that establishes a permanent connection for as long as that artifact exists, becoming for all intents and purposes an "Artifactal."

Let me also point out that these four do not include what I have called the "Elementals of Substance," such as subtle beings associated with plants, stones, water, earth, fire, and so on. These, as I indicated in the previous Field Note, are always present by the simple fact that our artifacts have to be made out of something and that something ultimately comes from the natural world. In the usual course of events, I don't think of them as techno-elementals because they do not normally interact with humanity in the way that techno-elementals do. This does not mean, though, that "natural elementals" or "elementals of substance" such as the spirits of wood or stone may not be curious about us or may not learn something from us, or that they may not be an influence upon us through our things. It's just that in the context of an artifact, they are usually not the dominant presence, their nature being subsumed in the hybridization occurring as their energy is joined with human thought and intent. It takes more of a deliberate intent to attune directly to an elemental of substance within an object that we have created.

This said, let's begin with the **artifactals** or "artifact elementals." These are the expression of the subtle life within our objects, given shape and identity by the purpose for which the artifact is made. They hold the energetic integrity and coherency of the artifact in question, as well as absorbing subtle energies through connection with the subtle environment around it.

Generally speaking, I understand these beings as taking the energetic, imaginal pattern of the artifact and holding it in clarity and stability so it can engage with the realm of substance and manifestation. Just as the nature elementals align with the consciousness of the Devas and other formative beings, so the artifactals have to align with the human energies of mind, feeling, and imagination. As I have said, this gives them a particular "spin" or "flavor" different from what is found in nature.

As I have described, the artifactal aligned with my Yoda figure is very simple. An artifactal aligned with my car is much more complex. In fact, given that my car is itself made up of many parts—or artifacts—it is really a collective of many different artifactals all aligned and collaborating within the field of the primary coordinating energy field of the car. (In a similar way, I can speak of my body elemental as coordinating the whole energetic field of my body but within it are discrete and discernible subtle intelligences associated with each of the major organs.)

In effect, subtle ecosystems within ecosystems!

An artifactal is in charge of the eight functions I described in Field Note #3: Identity, Organization, Energy Exchange, Metabolism, Generativity, Connection, *Holopoiesis*, and Emergence. How active these functions are in a given instance depends on the artifact, its uses, its ongoing involvement with human energy fields and activity, how "heightened" or energetically active and aware it is, and so on. For instance, until I added extra energy to its field through my love, my attention, my thought and imagination, my little Yoda had only minimal activity in most of these functions except for identity (as an object, not as "Yoda") and energetic organization.

It's in how these functions manifest in general that we find the main difference between an artifactal and an elemental and thus between the energetic fields of nature and those of the human built world. The function of both elemental and artifactal is to attune to and align with the will and purpose of a creative intelligence in order to assist something to come into being. In nature, though, the purposeful will of a Deva is itself attuned to the larger whole, the larger environment, in which the creative act is taking place. So, for instance, in manifesting the species of "maple tree," the Maple Tree Deva automatically is aware of how this tree will fit into the ecosystem in which it will become a member. In other words, the Deva creates holistically. The connective and holopoietic functions are active from the start; the maple tree becomes a participant in creating wholeness in its world because it knows itself to be part of that wholeness.

Further, the Deva is an agent of the evolution of consciousness. The maple tree is not a static creation but is capable of evolution and emergence. This function, too, is active from the beginning.

Human beings for the most part—at least at this stage of our consciousness development—are not so holistically aware. Human will is usually oriented exclusively to human purposes, needs and designs. Whereas the will of a Deva or angel is outward turned, aligning itself with the cosmos and with the Sacred, human will is inward and self-directed. This has become truer as our society has become more materialistic and industrialized.

To the Deva, everything is alive and everything is a subject with its own agency and sacredness. To the human, especially at this time in our history, only organic entities are alive, and most of those we treat not as subjects but as objects without regard to any intrinsic sacredness or subjectivity.

This means that an artifactal energy field created in tandem with human will may be weak and diminished when it comes to the functions of connection, *holopoiesis*, and emergence. Techno-elementals may have strong energetic identities and organization but be deficient in their ability to connect widely with the subtle worlds or participate in creating wholeness. Because we do not experience ourselves as connected to the larger world, the things we create are less likely to experience this connectedness themselves. This can have consequences that impact our human development and lives.

The second kind of techno-elemental is what I call a "**rider**." This is a subtle being who is attracted to humanity's energy and uses the energy field of one of our artifacts as a means of connecting with us. It may be curious about us and wish to sample our subtle energies and learn about this curious creature called a human being.

In my experience, subtle beings of many kinds, and in particular elementals, appear to be nourished and stimulated by the energy of will and purpose. In part this is because for many elemental beings, their function is aligned with translating creative will into form and manifestation. They are part of the Artisanal Force that brings the cosmos into expression.

Human technology may be understood as embodied intent or will. A tool is a manifestation of the will to do something. A hammer embodies the intent to build. A sword or gun embodies the intent to wound or kill, either in defense or offense. An automobile embodies the intent to travel. A printing machine embodies the will to produce writing on paper. Technology gives shape and form to a functional intent and is thus a "formative art" akin to what the spiritual formative forces of the world do.

Because of this, human technology is inherently of interest to certain kinds of elemental beings; it attracts them. The reasons for this attraction may be many. A rider may be attracted to the focused energy of will and intention. It may find energetic stimulation and nourishment from being around human fields of consciousness and activity. It may simply be curious about us. Learning is a powerful motivation in the subtle worlds; information and new experience is a powerful kind of "food" that can enhance the development of other forms of subtle life. Human beings are complex entities; we can hold and synthesize many different types of subtle energies in ways many simpler subtle organisms cannot. Learning how we do this by spending time in a humanly-generated energy field can be attractive.

In Field Note #1, I used the metaphor of action figures and points of articulation. As I said there, human consciousness is highly flexible; it can "bend" in a variety of ways. A being that has a less flexible or developed consciousness—one that has fewer "points of articulation"—may discover new capacities by observing the ways that we "bend." It might not have considered that "bending" in that manner was possible. In this way, engaging with us through the medium of our artifacts may be a way of enhancing the Emergence function, enabling that subtle organism to develop and advance in its own evolution.

Sometimes the attractive feature is simply to be in the presence and excitement of creative energy. I have a number of friends who are artists: writers, painters, actors, musicians. I love to be around them because they are charismatic. They have an aliveness that is attractive. In a similar way, we can be charismatic to subtle beings who are not as developed or creative as we are. Though we often create out of convenience or for purely commercial reasons, we also create out of inspiration, beauty, and joy. We manifest what I've been calling artisanal energies which nourish life and wholeness. In a learning universe, this is truly food to beings in the subtle realms. Riders may take up residence, so to speak, around something we've created to soak up the radiance we have brought into the world.

Some riders simply live within the energy field of the artifact, partaking of the energetic environment but not necessarily contributing much. Others actively augment the work of the artifactal, aligning with and supporting its purpose. This may be helpful, and, I think, usually is, but sometimes it can become problematic if the purpose of the artifact is energized in a way that overrides the will of its user. The focused energy and will of an elemental being can have a powerful and even a controlling effect upon a human whose own sense of sovereignty and wholeness is weak.

Not all riders come to feed or learn. There can be subtle beings who wish to be of service and use a connection with our artifacts as a way of doing so. I wrote earlier in Field Note #1 of the subtle being who attached itself to my oldest child's stuffed *Bumblelion* toy. When invoked, it would generate a loving, soothing field of energy.

Such beings become **allies**. They could be angels of one kind or another, Devas, disincarnate humans, nature spirits, or beings who don't conveniently fall into any of these categories (of which there are many in the ecology of the subtle worlds). What they all have in common is a desire to help in some way and an ability to use the energy field of a human artifact as a point of contact to do so.

Sometimes an artifact is created specifically to be a point of connection with a non-physical ally. An example of this is the "Sidhe Gate" created by my friend and Lorian colleague, Ron Hays. The Sidhe are spiritual "cousins" of humanity living in what for most purposes could be considered a subtle realm, though technically they are not subtle beings themselves. However, they can ally with us in various ways just the way a subtle being may do. (If you would like more information about these remarkable allies, Lorian produces *The Card*

Deck of the Sidhe created in collaboration with the Sidhe by Jeremy Berg and myself as well as two books, *Conversations with the Sidhe* and *Engaging with the Sidhe*.)

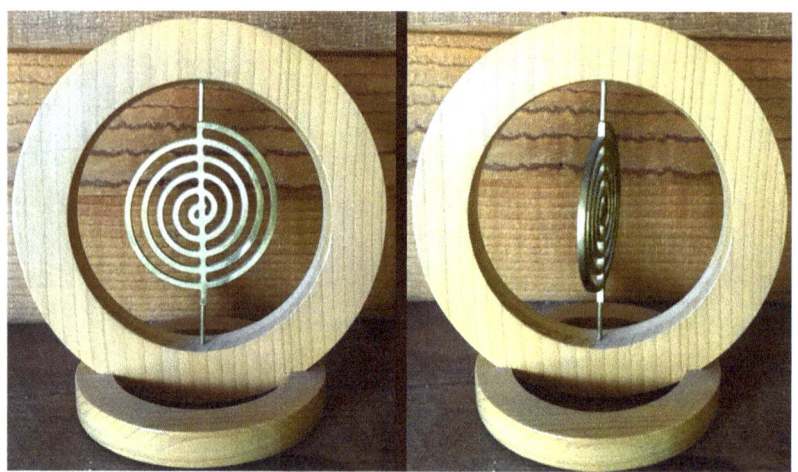

Handmade by Ron in his studio, the Sidhe Gate contains the Sidhe Glyph first presented by John Matthews in his excellent book, *The Sidhe*, as a meditative symbol for connecting with these beings. This glyph is mounted in such a way that it can turn, so that the "gate" can be open or closed. Ron creates these artifacts in attunement with his Sidhe allies so that each one can act as a point of contact with the energy field of the Sidhe realm. I have often used it to facilitate my own connection with these beings when it has been appropriate to do so. [If you would like information about these portable Sidhe Gates, Ron's website is elvengates.com]

Another, larger example of a subtle ally aligned with a particular artifact is the being I call my "House Angel." A house is definitely a human artifact, a product of our creative and technological skills, and like our bodies, it is a whole thing in itself while also containing a great many distinct parts. All houses—indeed, all buildings—have an energy field of their own which is influenced and shaped by their shape and function and also by what happens within them, the energetic activities which they contain. Like the "life-field" of any artifact, not all the eight functions may be in evidence or equally active. If the subtle field is not well developed, as is the case with many artifacts, it may exhibit a minimum of ability to connect, much less to be holopoietic or experience emergence. In other words, depending on the strength and activity of the field and the functions that are engaged and operating, it can exist anywhere along a wide spectrum of sentiency and interaction with human energy and consciousness.

In the case of my house, though, I have a daily practice of attuning to the overlighting sentiency of the structure, acknowledging and treating the life of my house as an ally and partner in my activity within and around the house. I consciously take time each day to link it through my own energy with the subtle energies in the natural environment, in particular the blessings radiated by the "Lady of the Lake" and by the surrounding mountains. As a consequence, in the subtle environment, the spirit of my house is very alive and present. It becomes an active conduit of blessing and spiritual energy for everything contained within the house and for all who enter it.

This segues into the fourth category of techno-elemental, the **sacramentals**. These are highly evolved spiritual beings, often angels or Devas of some nature, who use an artifact as a point of connection with us in order to transmit blessings or to offer energies that can enhance and nourish our own life and spiritual evolution. Such beings are often found overlighting (or at least attuned to) sacred buildings such as churches, synagogues, and mosques. But smaller artifacts can be aligned with such advanced spiritual allies as well. For instance, when I use my chalice as a sacramental object, it becomes a touch point for the energy of an angelic ally.

The difference between an "ally" and a "sacramental" is not always obvious; indeed, in many cases, they may be the same. But my rule of thumb is that an ally is a source of energetic assistance for everyday activity with which I may be engaged and is not necessarily concerned with or able to directly assist my spiritual development. It generally functions within the subtle environment in which I am living. A sacramental, on the other hand, is generally one of a class of beings, usually angelic in nature, that promote and assist our spiritual unfoldment and wholeness. It acts from a higher frequency of life beyond the subtle environment and works more through the inductive influence of presence than through the transmission of specific subtle energies.

It's important to remember that allies and sacramentals do not inhabit the artifacts with which they are connected. They may reside in their energy fields for a time if appropriate, but usually it has been my observation that they are linked to the energy of the artifact much as, say, a security company may be linked electronically to my home so that it is aware if an alarm goes off and can take action. The ally or sacramental can become aware and respond if the artifact to which it is linked "goes off" and sends an invocation.

For example, with my Sidhe Gate, the Sidhe don't live in it nor does simply rotating the metal glyph open my consciousness into their realm. I have to create that openness within myself though love, intention, attention, and presence. But it does serve as a lens to focus my intent to make contact. It acts as a talisman to give power to my desire and intent to connect with them. It "sets off an alarm," so to speak, that resonates into their realm. This may or may not actually produce a contact; nothing is being forced or coerced. But if all else is equal, then the presence of this "lens" or "gate" as an attuned artifact can facilitate the inner connection between my consciousness and that of a responding Sidhe.

The categories of artifactal, rider, ally, and sacramental are just my ways of classifying a realm of subtle organisms—the techno-elementals attracted to and influenced by our creations—that is itself a complex ecosystem. They are terms of convenience. Efforts at classification are hampered by the fact that boundaries are much more fluid and intermingling in the subtle realms than in the physical. It's easy to tell a pine tree from a maple tree; it's not as easy to distinguish a nature spirit from an elemental or an angel from a Deva. It takes careful discernment based on observation of function and a sensitivity to nuances of vibration and energy. Even with over sixty years of practice, I still can get it wrong.

Further, there are two other categories that I haven't included yet in this discussion but which play an increasingly powerful role in human affairs. These are the subtle beings associated with electricity and with the creation of cyberspace and artificial intelligence. They are different enough from the other four as to merit Field Notes of their own later in this book.

Though I've coined terms to describe these different categories of subtle beings, we have to be careful not to place more weight of meaning or significance upon them than they can bear. They are as much poetic as taxonomic terms. Being a "naturalist" of the subtle realms is as much art as it is science; my scientist friends would say it's more so!

One thing to keep in mind is that from the perspective of all subtle beings, from the simplest elemental to the most complex and evolved cosmic archangel, everything—and I do mean *everything*—is alive and sentient. All subtle beings live in a universe populated only by subjects. There are no "things." Everything is a "thou." Nothing is an "it." It is only we who can fail to appreciate this, and this is as much a failing of how we think and what we accept as reality as it is a matter of lacking the psychic abilities or talents to see the subtle realms. We lose ourselves in thought worlds of our own creation, mirror realms in which we see only ourselves and fail to see the immense wonder, depth, splendor, and above all, life of the larger world around us. It is this human tendency to create and live in our own artificial worlds of thought and belief, imagination and construction, that ultimately creates the problems, even dangers, that techno-elementals can pose.

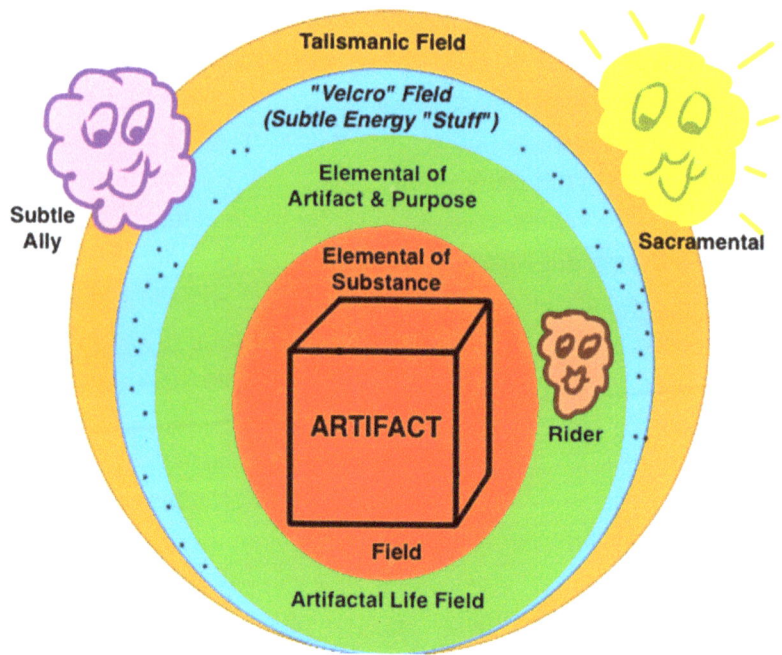

Figure 1
ARTIFACTAL ANATOMY: BASIC TECHNO-ELEMENTALS AND THEIR FIELDS OF SUBTLE ENERGY

For reference sake, Figure 1 provides a simple illustration of the techno-elementals and subtle energy fields I've discussed in this and the previous Field Note (note that in this diagram, the artifact has been "talismanized," hence it possesses a talismanic field that connects to an ally and a sacramental). This is an idealized picture. Not all artifacts have all four of the techno-elementals I've discussed present. All have artifactals, as well as elementals of substance. Beyond that, it depends on circumstances and on the nature of the artifact itself.

When I stand in my living room (acknowledging that it truly *is* a "living" room, a space filled with subtle life), the techno-elementals I perceive when I attune to them are as diverse as the different flowers in my wife's garden outside. For instance, there is a beautifully carved wooden end table between two of our sofas that belonged to my wife's great-grandmother and has been passed down through the generations to her grandmother, her mother, and now to her. It appears to be hand-crafted, most likely in the late Nineteenth Century, though at this point, we have no way of determining this. The artifactal I feel within it is like an elder. The energy around it is very calm and deep; in some ways, when I attune to it, it's like being in the presence of an old well. At the same time, I'm aware of a connection to a Rider, in this case the overlighting spirit or angel of my wife's maternal family line. This is not a strong presence, but it is there, like an old address or phone number that could, if desired, put one in touch with a distant relative. This connection or vibration rests within the energy field of this table like a blessing.

By contrast, there is a small, branching, metal candelabra that holds three candles resting on the mantle of the fireplace. I occasionally use these for simple rituals of lighting a candle for someone who is in need of blessing. When I do, a field develops around this artifact that is linked to a Sacramental, a spiritual ally that augments the blessing. Otherwise, though, the energy field around this candelabra is not particularly strong. I do not get a sense that its artifactal is particularly developed or sentient. If the artifactal of the table is old, this one is very young.

In other words, some of the objects and artifacts in my living room have strong fields and are an energetic presence while others do not and are not. A few have Riders or, at times, Sacramentals; most do not. The point is that techno-elementals are every bit as diverse as every other form of life on earth. In this book, I am generalizing about them in order to keep things simple, but this is like talking about plants as a single category when we all know that in the world, plants manifest in a bewildering and wondrous array of different species.

FIELD NOTE 11: FROM TALISMAN TO TECH

Human beings shape their environment all the time. What our modern culture has largely forgotten is that we are also always shaping a non-physical, subtle environment as well. The emergence of techno-elementals is a consequence of this activity.

At the Findhorn Foundation Community in northern Scotland, the gardeners have worked miracles in the community gardens through attuning to and cooperating with the elementals and nature spirits associated with the soil and with various plant species. Our ancestors worked in much the same way. In times past, humans have sought the help of subtle beings in growing crops, in hunting, in healing, in weather-working, and in general assistance for the tribe or clan. In fact, agriculture can be seen as one of the earliest, if not *the* earliest, form of human technology, in which case the first techno-elementals may well have been nature spirits adapting to and cooperating with the creation of cultivated plants and farms.

Similarly, early craftspersons would do their weaving, their blacksmithing, their pottery-making, and other arts in a way that would often invoke subtle presences and qualities in the process. This might be done through prayer, ritual, song, dance, imaginative visualization, or other means of attunement and alignment. Because all of the substances that humans used to build and to make their tools came from nature, the original techno-elementals were essentially spirits and elementals of nature, as I have described. Put another way, the human world and the natural world were not as segregated as they are today (at least in our thinking), nor were the subtle and physical dimensions as separated in people's awareness. However, as the human realm became more distinctly human in both subtle and physical ways and the boundaries between our world and that of nature became more pronounced, the subtle beings associated with our crafts and technology began to differentiate from their nature cousins as well.

For instance, many of the nature spirits and elementals engaging with humanity, including with our agriculture and gardens, began to mimic our human form, at least to some extent (something easy for a subtle being to do whose energy form allows it to shapeshift). In my experience, many nature spirits I've encountered have no particular form that I can see; they appear to me as swirling ribbons or points of Light; but I have also seen them take on human form as sometimes it can be easier for me to relate to something that looks like me rather than to a formless radiance.

In a broad, sweeping way, we can track the development of techno-elementals along a developmental arc that roughly parallels the development of human civilization and its increasing differentiation and separation from the natural world. In the beginning, there was little difference between a spirit or elemental aligned with nature and one associating with human enterprise and creativity. Over time, at least the "artifactals" became more and more influenced and shaped by human consciousness and intent rather than by the Devic and angelic energies that overlight and flow through all the natural world.

For convenience sake, I track this emergence of techno-elementals in terms of four stages of human consciousness and intentionality. I call these stages **Integrated, Aligned, Divorced**, and **Disconnected**. These four describe a developmental arc from a close relationship to the natural and subtle worlds to one that is separated and distinct. As long as we realize that they are rough generalizations and that neither human nor subtle world activity can be neatly categorized in discrete boxes, I think these stages can help us understand the challenge that techno-elementals can pose, which in the end is the challenge of our own states of consciousness.

By **integrated**, I mean that the humans involved at this stage feel themselves integrated with nature, not separate from it. They act with awareness of and in partnership with the subtle life and energies of the natural world. People felt themselves spiritually and energetically as well as physically part of the land on which they lived, hunted, farmed and built. For all practical purposes, human intent was not far removed from Devic or angelic intent. While more universally common in our ancestral past, there are certainly people who live this way today. The gardeners at Findhorn, for instance, consciously seek to be integrated and collaborative with the spiritual intelligences that are part of the subtle life of the garden. It was not a far reach for an elemental or nature spirit to connect with human intent and still feel connected to the larger Devic and angelic realms of nature.

As civilizations developed and the human world began to take on its own unique characteristics separate from the natural world around it, tools and artifacts developed their own distinct identities and energies. A woven blanket, a sword or hammer fresh from the blacksmith's forge, a chair from a carpenter's shop, and a cup newly formed on a potter's wheel were something new in the world. They emerged from human imagination, intent and skill, not from the operation of natural forces. One couldn't plant a seed and have a rug or a table sprout from the land.

As I said earlier, many of the early craftspersons saw the creation of such artifacts as a magical act, and they would invoke spiritual assistance or allies in the crafting process. This is what I think of as a stage of **alignment**. The weavers, blacksmiths, carpenters, potters, and so forth were aligning their creative work with subtle energies and subtle beings, much as I might invoke a "rider" to align with my child's stuffed animal or my friend called upon the Sidhe to align with the Sidhe Gate he was making.

This alignment may not have been as deeply connected with the subtle worlds as occurred with those whose consciousness was more integrated with the natural world, but connection was still there. The beings who aligned with human creativity in these instances were increasingly shaped and influenced by human thought and intent but they were still being acknowledged and respected as part of a larger subtle ecosystem. They were techno-elementals, but the will and desire of the craftsperson to be in alignment with that larger spiritual world in the act of creating meant they had one foot in each realm, so to speak, the human and the natural.

A particularly powerful form of this aligned intent takes the form of creating *talismans*. I understand a talisman to be any artifact deliberately aligned with and attuned to a specific subtle energy or being. It imbues an object with special energetic and spiritual properties and attributes, heightening the living energy field of the artifact and enhancing its sentiency and interactivity with its environment. In effect, it gives that artifact a clearer, more distinct sense of identity and purpose. It is also a customary way of invoking an ally or a "sacramental" to link with a particular object. My chalice is an example of this.

A talisman is particularly powerful when it is created as such from the start, with each stage of its crafting from raw material to finished artifact being blessed and infused with intentional alignment with the desired spiritual forces and subtle allies. This is what my friend did in creating my Sidhe Gate.

However, it's quite possible to take any artifact and "talismanize" it. I could, for instance, do this with my Yoda figure. I would have to determine if I simply wanted to link it with an ally or a general subtle quality, as I did with my child's stuffed animal, or if I want it linked to a "sacramental", an angelic or Devic consciousness. The latter is a more intense operation. If I were to do that, it would require more energy and focus on my part. It's not a casual thing to do, any more than becoming consecrated and ordained as a minister or priest is a casual act. There are consequences and commitments that result. As a matter of personal practice, I would never link an object with a "sacramental" without first asking its permission and gaining the cooperation of its inherent life, for this kind of sacred alignment can profoundly alter the energy field of the object.

The main point I wish to make here is that if I create or treat an artifact with a consciousness and intent born of a sense of alignment, I create a subtle environment in which any techno-elemental associated with that artifact, either as an artifactal, a rider, an ally, or a sacramental, is connected not only with human energy but with a larger spiritual context as well.

Over time, though, human awareness has generally moved further and further from a ready knowledge and attunement to the subtle realms, replacing familiarity with ignorance, fear, or disbelief. We have become ever more focused on human life as fundamentally removed and distinct from the world of nature. All of nature has lost its personhood in our eyes. Animals, plants, landscapes, rivers, lakes, all became objects for humanity's use.

Consequently, the intent behind the design and making of our artifacts and tools became more **divorced** from any alignment with spiritual qualities or subtle energies. Given that human beings can channel artisanal forces, loving and blessing what they are making even without knowledge of the subtle worlds, such human-oriented creative intention can still carry a spiritual force with it. But it is no longer automatically connected to the larger ecosystem of the planet's wholeness. In the way that a dog is different from a wolf, even though both are canines, the subtle beings involved with human creativity became more and more "domesticated" and shaped by the characteristics of human consciousness and energy. Increasingly, there came into being subtle organisms adapted to living as part of the subtle environment of the human world. Techno-elementals became energetically distinguishable from their natural cousins.

I have found this distinction even extends into the angelic and Devic realms. The angel of a city is not the same as the Deva of a forest, even though they may perform a similar function of overlighting a specific domain and environment of life with blessing and spiritual empowerment.

With the beginning of the Industrial Revolution, mass production came into being on a scale never before experienced. Increasingly, the manufacture of goods and products shifted from home- and village-based enterprises and handicrafts to the use of machines, steam power, assembly lines, and factories. Although human creativity and design are still present (at least until recently when artifacts began to be designed and produced by artificial digital intelligences), the actual assembly and making of objects required less and less direct human involvement as methods of automation evolved. Oversight might be needed, but this is a different kind of awareness and energy than that invoked by actual creative intent and engagement.

I think of this state, in which much of the modern world now exists, as **disconnected**. We are still part of the natural world, but we have been acting as if we are not. This sense of division and disconnection cannot help but affect those subtle beings whose lives are integrated and associated with our own, the techno-elementals. It creates conditions in which many of these beings cannot express their full potential and become quiescent and dormant, diminishing the health and vitality of the subtle environments in which we live. We are the poorer for it.

Again, I want to stress that these four stages are generalizations. There are human beings all around the modern world who have a deep appreciation for and attunement to nature and the subtle dimensions. There are buildings and other artifacts crafted with love and awareness that are fully connected to the flow of healthy, subtle energies moving through the spiritual realms. Not all techno-elementals are disconnected from their "wilder cousins" or from the spiritual worlds. Yet, at the same time, we have to acknowledge that many aspects of modern civilization are truly removed and disconnected. With the advent of virtual reality, augmented reality, artificial intelligence, and other digital technologies, we are on the brink of even more isolation in realms fashioned purely from human imagination divorced from the larger physical, subtle, and spiritual environments.

Up to now, I've been writing in terms of subtle energies and their flow within the subtle environment close to the physical realm. These are living energies that bring vitality and connection to everything that exists in material form. But there's another dimension at work here, one that may appropriately be called spiritual, a depth dimension in which life affects life not through currents and flows of subtle energies but through resonance and presence.

Our creativity is a manifestation of our inner life, a life of soul as well as of mind and emotion. When our inner life is expansive and "warm," filled with a loving connection to the world, this living, spiritual warmth or radiance embraces and, in a sense, ensouls all that we create. We fill even our most utilitarian, practical tools with a loving quality I might call "soul-warmth." Even if we have no awareness of the innate spiritual life within our things, our own inner life, when resonant with joy and lovingness, blesses that artifactal life even as we shape its subtle energies and its physical forms.

But when our inner life is constricted, alienated, "cold," bereft of joy or warmth of soul, then there is no warmth radiated to the things we create. They may be beautiful in form, but they lack the blessing of our own soul-warmth. They become cold as well. This is the result when what we create is born of selfishness and a utilitarian attitude that turns everything into a means and not an end in itself. In such a situation, we do not vivify the thing-in-itself but make its identity conditional to fulfilling our own purposes. Such purposes may contain no spark of care for the good of others or for humanity, or the world, but are constrained by the limits of personal greed. This greed may not be for money; it could be for power or for acclaim, but the pull is inward towards an isolated self and not outward in contribution to a larger whole.

There have always been people who have brought the qualities of a rich, loving, active inner life to their outer lives, especially to their creative endeavors. There have always been people who have not. But as the arc of human civilization has moved further and further into a materialistic mindset, one that sees the natural world simply as a resource to be exploited and not as a partner, our collective incarnate soul life has been dwindling. This affects the inner life of the world we create, which has a reciprocal effect upon our own.

A materialist world-view that leads us to deny or ignore the inner life of the world around us—and in particular, of the artifacts we create—is not the only challenge we face. We are also confronted now with an entirely new "species" of elemental consciousness and energy that has become intimately interwoven with our lives. These are the techno-elementals of electricity.

FIELD NOTE 13: FRANKLIN'S KEY

In the summer of 1752, Benjamin Franklin attached a metal key to the moistened string of a kite and flew it into a thunderstorm. When it was struck by lightning and sparks jumped from the key to his hand, he knew that lightning and electricity were the same thing.

Although the phenomenon of electricity has been known for millennia, it wasn't studied scientifically until the middle of the 1600's. Even then, a hundred years passed before its characteristics began to be understood and it began to be taken seriously as more than just a curiosity; Franklin was one of the prime movers in this shift of attitude and attention. His experiments paved the way for an intensification of scientific and practical investigation into electrical phenomena which opened the door to exciting technological possibilities.

The first practical application of this new understanding was the invention and development of the telegraph in 1840. It was not long before telegraph wires became a common part of the technological landscape. In 1872 a dynamo that converted mechanical energy into electrical energy was developed, which led to the modern electrical power industry. The first major use of this energy was in lighting through the use of arc lights. A rapid expansion of this application came when Thomas Edison invented the light bulb in 1880. It was Edison—the "Wizard of Menlo Park"—who truly inaugurated the new electrical age, flinging wide the door which Franklin's key had unlocked.

The effect of this new technology has been to create an environment unlike any other in which human beings have lived before. Sitting here at my desk writing these words, I am immersed in that electronic environment. Apart from the obvious presence of my computer, I have nearby a printer, a CD player, and lamps. Electrical wires are in all the walls around me throughout the house. In other rooms are other electrical devices, such as a television, more lights, another computer, an electric stove and oven, and telephones. Outside my house are streetlights and telephone and cable wires. My neighborhood, though, is filled with trees. If I lived in a city, I would be even more surrounded by electrical devices, energies, and fields.

Of course, this doesn't even mention all the electromagnetic waves penetrating my house from television and radio broadcasts and from satellite connections with our cell phones.

At one time, the dominant environment was the natural world. Even living in cities, people were not far from the realms of nature, and of course, their building materials of stone, marble, wood, and metal call came from that environment.

But since the invention of the telegraph, the electronic environment has grown and grown, especially since end of the Second World War and with even greater rapidity in the past thirty years as electronic technology has become more sophisticated, miniaturized, ubiquitous, and powerful. Now if our electrical energy were cut off, our civilization would collapse. For the first time in our history, we are dependent on an environment other than the natural one. The electromagnetic environment has become the dominant feature in our lives. Furthermore, this has not happened through slow evolution over hundreds of years. It has happened in the blink of an eye in geological time. It is as if we went to bed in one world and awoke in another, wholly different one.

Up to now in this book, the techno-elementals I've been discussing—and the ones with which I have the most experience—have been part of humanity's life and experience for millennia. In a sense, we and they have grown up together. Electricity is part of nature, too, but until the beginning of the Twentieth Century, other than lightning, it was not part of the environment that most people experienced. Now it is a major element (if not the dominant feature) of the environment in which three-quarters of humanity live.

There is a major difference between the techno-elementals I've been describing and the subtle intelligences and energies associated with electricity, which I might refer to as "Electro-Elementals." For one thing, electricity is not a substance in the same way that stone, metal, plastic, and wood are. It's a force. In fact, it's an expression of one of the four fundamental forces in the universe: gravity, electromagnetism, and the strong and weak nuclear forces. Electro-elementals are a pure expression of a subtle presence and energy that is a universal force.

In their interaction with humanity, electro-elementals are not hybrids. They are not a blend with human energies and intent the way the artifactals are. Like water or fire, we can direct electricity and utilize it, but it remains its own thing. We do not shape it in the way we shape wood or stone, metal or clay. We adapt to it rather than the other way around.

I have not had as much experience tuning in to the subtle nature of electricity or of electro-elementals. I am aware of their affect upon our own energy fields, but it has been harder for me to touch into them directly in the way I have done with other techno-elementals. I can only offer a series of impressions; much more research and inner investigation needs to be done in this area. Hopefully, these impressions will be helpful to others who feel called to explore in this area.

Because electricity is a force—a current of energy—and not a substance, there is no physical object that I could see or touch to make an initial point of contact and resonance (I was not about to handle a live electrical wire!). I don't touch fire, either, to connect to it, but at least I can light a candle and be in the presence of a flame. Electricity, though, is all around me in one form or another (including within my own body in the bioelectric activity of my cells). To have a focal point for my initial investigation, I chose an electric socket in the wall of my house and projected my consciousness into it.

At first, I made no contact with anything (though I was aware of the artifactals in the wall of the house). But eventually, I found my consciousness in touch with a vast presence that seemed to extend endlessly into the void of space. What was interesting is that it was not in itself particularly energetic; it really did feel like a cold, impersonal void. It was not an inviting contact at first, though there was nothing overtly inimical or negative about it. It just felt inhuman in a way that even the elemental presences of stone and fire, water and air do not.

I repeated this exercise several times, each time coming a bit more into resonance with this Presence. As I grew more familiar with it, I no longer needed to use the electrical socket as a point of imaginal contact but could move directly into connection with this cosmic Life.

When I first recounted my contact with this Presence in the earlier version of this book (published as a special issue of my esoteric journal, *Views from the Borderland*), I spoke of encountering a "cold sun," a source of impersonal Light that seemed very "mental" to me, lacking the warmth of the spiritual Light of our sun. It seemed to me at the time that the influence of this "cold sun" of electro-elemental consciousness could be damaging to humans, drawing out and emphasizing a coldness of intellect not balanced with the love of the heart.

However, I subsequently realized as I pursued this investigation that this was an incomplete observation. I simply had not gone deeply enough into contact with the fullness of this Being, this Angel or Deva of electricity and electromagnetism. It was impersonal, yes, but once I'd gotten past that, I discovered a loving presence that was warm and welcoming in its own way.

What I eventually touched into was a sense of service to life. As one of the foundational forces of the physical universe, it is necessary for physical life to exist. It has no attachment to any particular form that that life may take (organic or inorganic), hence the feeling of impersonality, but it is attached in a loving way to Life itself and its manifestation.

Further, it seemed directly involved with the processes by which creative impulses originating in higher frequencies of mind and spirit become manifest in the physical universe; that is, it is related to the process of manifestation itself, providing subtle energies or pathways for ideas to take form and substance.

Are there elementals of electricity and electromagnetism in the same way there are elementals of fire and water, earth and air? Yes, I believe so. I've had students who have seen them looking like "Reddi Kilowatt," the stick-figure whose body is made of lightning bolts and whose head is a light bulb, designed by Ashton B. Collins, Sr. in 1926 to advertise the Alabama Power Company. I've never seen them looking like this, though it doesn't surprise me as I know subtle beings can take on forms shaped by images in our imaginations. My impression, though, is that such electro-elementals are usually not so distinct and formed but are more like points of consciousness that arise out of the electrical flow for one purpose or another and then merge back into it. They do not normally seem as capable of independent existence as, say, an elemental of stone, but this may simply be a limitation of my own perception.

On the other hand, I have felt a strong emanation of curiosity when I attune to the electro-elemental domain. These are beings—or at least a field of consciousness—that historically have not been directly involved with humanity, other than at a cellular, biological level. Now, within less than two hundred years, they have been thrust into close and continuing contact with us. It's as if two alien species have come together in the depths of space and are trying to understand each other and how they might relate. I have a sense of electro-elementals taking special forms to study and understand our mode of life, so different from their own, in order to interact with us more creatively. They are adjusting, to the extent they are able.

As an example of this, one morning I was sitting in my living room when a subtle being appeared to my inner sight. It was vaguely human shaped, even feminine in its form. At first, I thought its body was black in color, then I realized that it wasn't black as much as it was void of any color, at least of any color I could perceive. However, around its shape was a flickering blue-white rim that outlined it to my vision. In a way, it was like looking through a portal in human form into the darkness of interstellar space.

It sounds foreboding as I write about it, but in fact, the presence of this being was friendly and reassuring. It definitely had a feminine feel to its vibration. It said that it was an emanation from the electrical field created by all the electricity running through my house, whether from the wires in the walls or from all the appliances that I have that work through electricity, from our computers to our television, from the electric stove to the many lamps throughout the house, and so on. It was quite explicit that it was not attached to any single artifact but to the electrical field itself. It was, it said, "born from the flow of electric current throughout the house." In this, it reminded me very much of a water elemental that arises from the flowing river itself and does not belong to any one segment of it.

It said that it was there as a point of contact between the elemental domain of "electricals" or electro-elementals and me. I had the distinct impression it was a form created in response to my reaching out by the deeper spiritual (angelic or Devic) Intelligence behind the phenomenon of electricity to provide a point of contact that was easier for my human consciousness to apprehend and to connect to. Just as my computer mouse and keyboard allow me to communicate with the machine intelligence of my computer, which otherwise is incomprehensible to me, so this subtle being was a kind of "UI" or User Interface. It was there to make it easier to contact its otherwise very inhuman realm of consciousness.

This contact happened while I was working on this book, and I have not had the opportunity of pursuing it any further. But I shall do so in the future, as there is much more to learn about and from this potential elemental ally.

There is another aspect to this investigation. If I compare the energy field around my chalice or my Yoda statue with that around my lamp or my computer printer, the latter have an additional layer of subtle energy related to the presence of electricity as part of their makeup and function. In this sense, especially in highly technological electronic artifacts, the artifactal connected to that object is itself being influenced by the presence of electrical energy and its subtle aspects. It is being "electrified" in a way, becoming a new kind of hybrid, one that now incorporates aspects of the electro-elemental domain as well as that of its own artifactal nature.

This holds true for the conduction of electrical currents. We do not use "free electricity" such as lightning; we utilize conductive materials, like copper wire, to hold and transmit the electrical current (although the Austrian electrical engineer Nikolas Tesla did demonstrate early in the Twentieth Century that electricity could be safely transmitted wirelessly). This means that an electro-elemental may appear to us demonstrating characteristics of the physical substance that is conducting it.

For this reason, I have realized upon further investigation and observation that some of the beings that I originally took to be electro-elementals are instead "electrified artifactals." Their consciousness and energy is heightened not only by association and blending with human energies but with engagement with the electricity that they contain or that energizes them. Their artifactal energy becomes a conduit for the expression of the electro-elemental life. When I attune to this, I have the impression that the "electrified artifactal" embodies the living field of the object itself while enabling electro-elementals to act as permanent "riders" attached to the object.

To finish this Field Note, here is a repeat of the simple illustration of the techno-elementals and subtle energy fields I presented earlier in the book. All is the same except in this case, I have added the electro-elemental field with its points of electro-elemental consciousness.

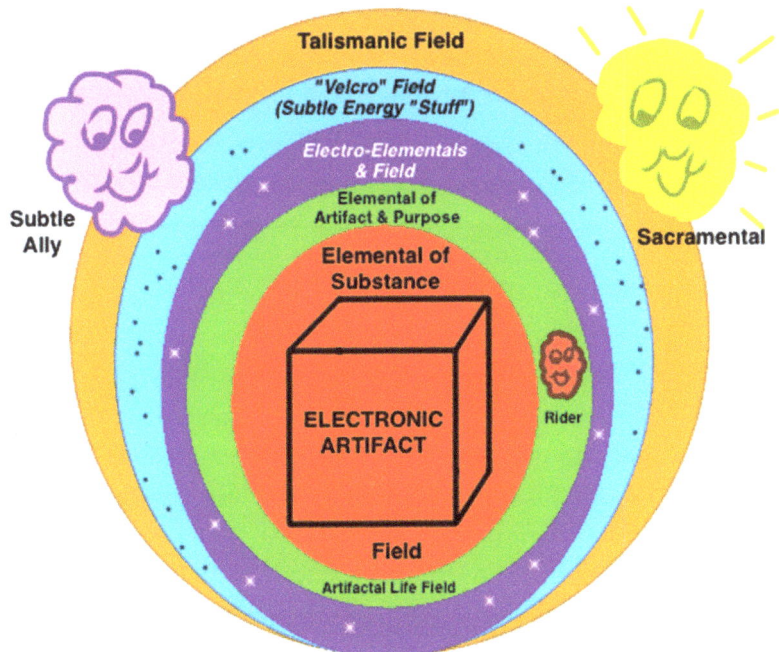

Figure 2:
ARTIFACTAL ANATOMY: BASIC TECHNO-ELEMENTALS
AND THEIR FIELDS OF SUBTLE ENERGY,
INCLUDING THE ELECTRO-ELEMENTALS

FIELD NOTE 13: THE GRAIL OF EVOLUTION

To fully appreciate the situation in which we find ourselves with techno-elementals, I need to bring to your attention an important phenomenon in the life and evolution of subtle organisms, at least as I perceive and understand them. This applies to all subtle organisms, whether we're talking about elementals, nature spirits, Devas, angels, or techno-elementals. It even applies to us, though we are so conditioned to see the world through the lens of our individuality, particularly in Western culture, that it is not immediately apparent.

Simply put, in the subtle realms, all evolution is collective in nature. The individual subtle organism may heighten and intensify its particular nature and function through experience and stimulation, but evolution occurs through webs and networks of relationship. Put another way, evolution doesn't happen in a vacuum.

To explain this, let me return to the Eight Functions I discussed in Field Note 5. They are Identity, Organization, Exchange, Metabolism, Generativity, Connection, *Holopoiesis*, and Emergence. All subtle organisms possess all eight functions to one degree or another, as we've already seen.

These eight functions can be grouped into four areas. Identity and Organization work internally at the core of the consciousness to establish the basic nature and beingness of the subtle organism. So I could think of them as acting within an "internal circle" of focus and intention, a circle that provides the overall function of Holding for the organism, that is to say, holding it in its unique nature and function.

Exchange, Metabolism, and Generativity are together "subtle physiological" functions that not only maintain the subtle organism in balance and health but also in interaction with its environment. I think of this as an "external circle" of processing and interaction.

However, the exchanges that occur at this "subtle physiological" level are very basic, such as the taking in of energetic nourishment and the generation of subtle energies in return. This occurs essentially automatically, the energy field of the subtle organism absorbing what it needs from the surrounding subtle environment and returning subtle energy to it in return.

To activate the last three functions of connection, *holopoiesis*, and emergence requires intention. It is not automatic, though it can be assisted. They are expressions of love in action accompanied with a will to connect, a will to create wholeness, and a will to evolve.

When intention creates a connection and a *holopoietic* relationship—that is, the connecting subtle organisms are seeking to create wholeness between them—then something else comes into being. It is the product of a co-creative synergy in which the whole is greater than just the sum of its parts. What I call a "space" or a field of subtle presence, energy, and possibility comes into being. It is this field that facilitates emergence, the unfoldment and appearance of something new or an evolutionary change. In effect, a potential held within the Generative Mystery—the presence of God—now has a space and an opportunity to reveal itself. The "figures slumbering in the stone" are set free.

I call this space or field of emergence "Grail Space." Learning to create Grail Space in our environment is one of the central practices of Incarnational Spirituality. It is a "space" or condition that facilitates spiritual progress, unfoldment, and evolution for all participating in its creation. In the Christian tradition, the Holy Grail is the vessel that held the blood of Christ and thus the presence and qualities of the Sacred. I call this field of emergence "Grail Space" in honor of this idea because it also is a vessel that holds the evolutionary power of the Sacred, the intent of the Sacred to make Itself known through the instrumentality of creation.

I illustrate these eight functions and the relationships that create Grail Space and Emergence in Figure 3.

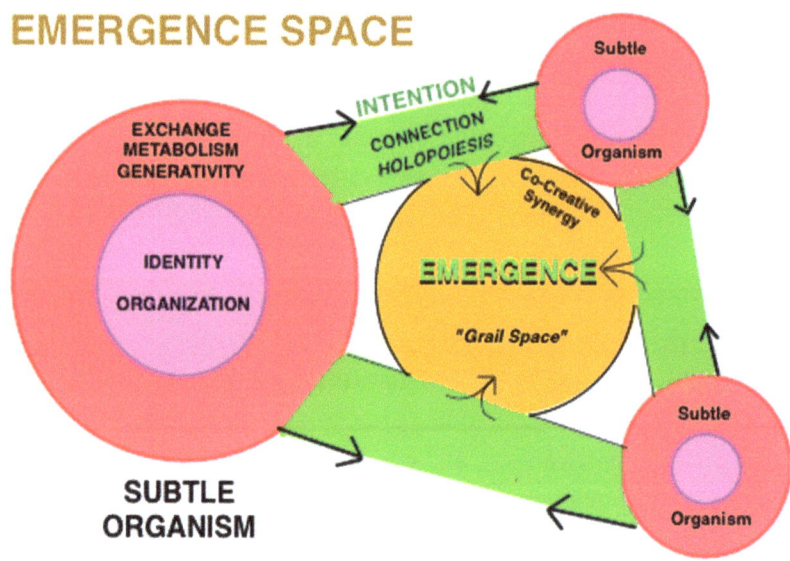

FIGURE 3
Emergence as a Shared Function

Most elementals and artifactals are either simple in their internal make-up or focused on a particular task. Either condition makes them unable to generate on their own the intention and energy necessary to form the holopoietic connections that enable Grail Space to emerge. They require help to do so, and this help normally comes from higher frequencies of consciousness such as nature spirits, Devas, and angels. More complex subtle organisms are capable of generating a field of emergence or Grail Space internally as they are themselves living systems of relationship and connection that can form the necessary connections, and they can produce the quality of will and love that is necessary to do so. This means part of their evolution can be internal and self-generated. But there are levels of evolution that even the most advanced Being cannot accomplish on its own but only in cooperation and co-creative synergy with others.

As incarnated human beings, we also are essentially complex subtle organisms, at least in the non-physical dimensions of our nature. Each of us is a blend of four different levels of functioning: the physical or physiological, the psychological, the spiritual, and the subtle energetic. All four of these make essential contributions to our overall health and well-being and are part of the web of internal relationships that form our whole, integrated incarnational system. It is this system that can, when properly activated by intention and love, create our own inner Grail Space, a key practice in our own spiritual evolution.

What is important to realize is that no organism, subtle or physical, is isolated from its environment. Therefore, the integration and wholeness of any being needs to include its relationship and interactions with the world around it. I illustrate this is Figure 4. Note that every element in this system touches upon and affects in some manner every other element. These connections and interactions can be obstructed or diminished. For example, I could live in my mind, ignoring my body, my soul, and my subtle energy field, paying minimal attention to the world around me. Or I might focus exclusively upon my physical and psychological well-being, ignoring the subtle side of my nature and ignoring the welfare of others in my environment. I might, on the other hand, pay too much attention to my non-physical side, becoming excessively ascetic and seeking to "overcome" or even eliminate my personality, thereby allowing the health and development of my mind, my emotions, and body to suffer.

All of these efforts to privilege one side of our nature over the others—or to go to extremes either in selfishness, ignoring the world, or in service, ignoring ourselves—will damage our integration and wholeness, making the unfoldment of an inner Grail Space less likely.

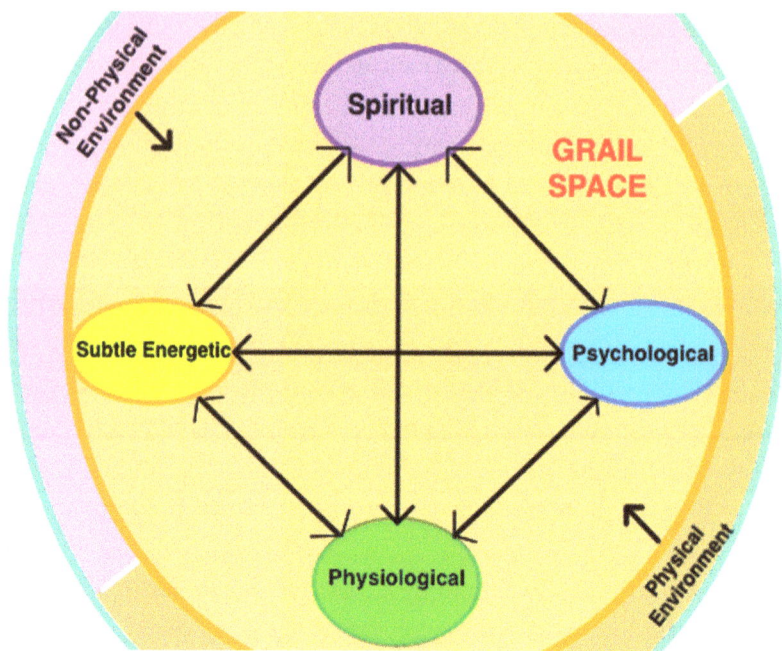

FIGURE 4
An Integrated System of Incarnation Forming a Grail Space

An objective in Incarnational Spirituality is to honor these five elements (counting the environment) and the co-creative relationships between them. With loving intention and attention, we can create a state of wholeness within ourselves and between ourselves and our environment that brings Grail Space into being both internally and around us. I write about this in detail in my books *Journey into Fire* and *Partnering with Earth*.

To achieve this, we have to transcend the materialistic worldview so common in our culture. We are not taught to see ourselves in wholeness. Aspects of our nature are left out. For the most part, our society is focused primarily on the interactions of just the psychological and the physiological elements. While for many, the spiritual dimension is a major and important factor in their lives, it is often presented in ways that make it seem distant or difficult to attain. As for the subtle energetic side of our nature, this remains largely unknown, ignored, or misunderstood.

Another stumbling block can be learning to understand the value of both the individual and the group. There is a natural limit to how far any being, no matter how advanced, can evolved on its own. Evolution is a collective endeavor. We cannot transcend this limit without forming loving and holopoietic connections with the world around us. This is certainly true at the soul level where our souls function in mutually supportive evolutionary clusters and groups—in effect in "soul-created Grail Spaces." If spiritual and consciousness development is our goal, then we need each other and we need the world in all its dimensions.

Looked at from "the top down," so to speak, the whole universe, with all its interconnections, interrelationships, entanglements, and interdependencies is a cosmic Grail Space, a grail of evolution, in which and through which the Sacred is emerging. The principle of evolution through connection runs the gamut from galaxy to atom.

This process is dynamic. New connections and relationships are constantly being discovered and formed, some existing only a short time, some lasting for eons. When patterns of connection outlive their usefulness, they are dissolved and connections broken, allowing something new to form and take its place. As this happens, grail spaces disappear and new grail spaces emerge.

Yet at times, connections are dimmed or broken that should not be. A grail can be shattered, its space dispersed or never properly formed before it has fulfilled its function. Emergence is blocked or denied. In such situations, life is not living up to its full potentials.

This is the situation affecting many of the techno-elementals in relationship to humanity. Understanding why this is so allows us to understand the challenges that the techno-elementals pose as well as the means for resolving them. This is what we will explore in the next Field Note.

FIELD NOTE 14: THE BROKEN BRIDGE

In Field Note 6, I discussed what I called the "artisanal" forces at work in the world. The definition of an artisanal force is not simply that it creates but that it does so embodying the love, the joy, and holopoietic qualities of the Sacred. Ultimately what the artisanal forces create foster and contribute to manifesting wholeness in the universe, revealing the unity and oneness of the Generative Mystery.

The artisanal forces of Gaia manifest through the Devas, nature spirits, and elementals. One result of their efforts is the natural world that we experience. Humanity at the soul level is an artisanal force as well, manifesting through the imagination, purpose, and skill of incarnate humans. One result of our efforts is the whole realm of our artifacts, from paper clips and sofas to cyclotrons and test tubes, and from jumbo jets to computers and office buildings.

As I've described, these artifacts manifest in the subtle realms as hybrid subtle organisms, the artifactals and the associated riders, allies, and, at times, sacramentals that together make up the larger category of techno-elementals.

In an ideal world, the realms of human artifacts would be a new form of "hybrid nature," and the techno-elementals would be simply another type of elemental or nature spirit. They would act as a bridge of connection and communion between the human and natural worlds, as well as between Gaian and human artisanal forces. Such a relationship would look like this:

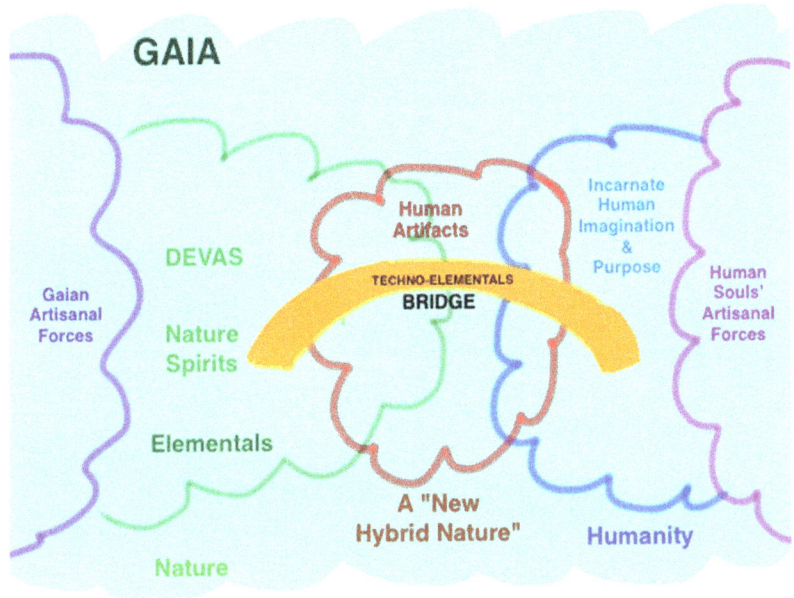

FIGURE 5
The Techno-Elemental "Bridge"

As this picture suggests, all the participants in these various planetary physical and subtle ecosystems are held within the life-field of Gaia, the World Soul, and all contribute to its evolution and wholeness. The Earth becomes an expression of partnership and co-creation between the spiritual nature and potentials of humanity and the spiritual nature of the world. What we create may reflect human needs and purposes but it is integrated energetically with the environments around us, both physical and subtle.

This integration means that the life-forces flowing from the spiritual forces and intelligences within nature—the Devas, the nature spirits, and so forth—have clear access to the life embodying itself within human artifacts. I can illustrate this by referring to a revised version of Figure 3 from the previous Field Note:

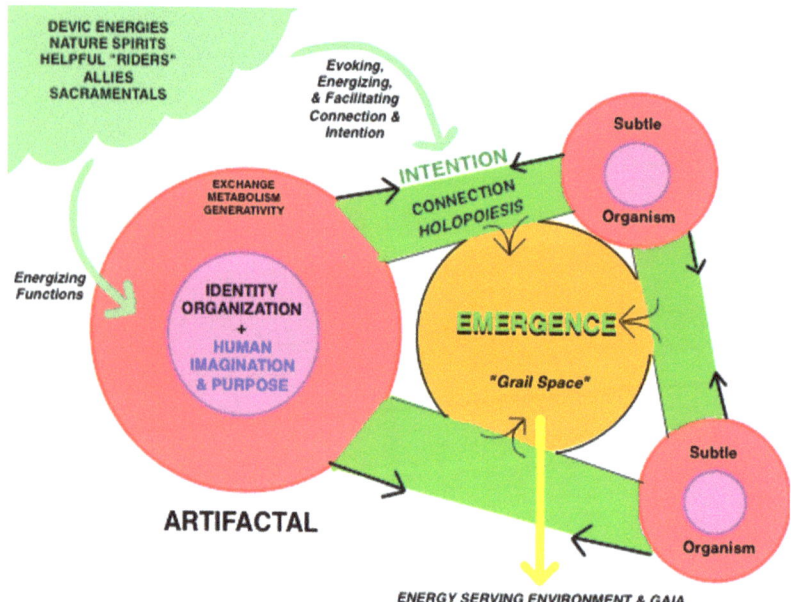

FIGURE 6
A Connected, Integrated State

The artifactal embodies the eight primary functions, as we have discussed earlier, but in this case, its identity is blended with the human imagination and purpose that gave form, structure, and function to whatever kind of artifact it is (and understand that this is a very simplified, generic schematic of subtle energy relationships).

What is important is that in this connected state, there is a flow of subtle energies of various kinds into the artifactal from different appropriate sources in the subtle realms. This flow is stimulating and nourishing to the expression of its functions, enhancing its vitality and life. If it is a simple subtle organism, as many artifactals are, then this flow may also draw forth, energize and facilitate that intention that creates the kind of holopoietic connections necessary to bring grail space into being. Otherwise, if the artifactal is more complex because it is embodying a complex structure, machine or artifact, then it may be able to produce this from within itself. But even then, it is assisted by the vitalization and stimulation provided by connection with the overall Devic realms of nature and Gaia.

In turn, this vitalization and emergence leads the artifactal to radiate its own energy, its own "self-Light," that can bless and energetically serve both its local environment and the larger wholeness of Gaia itself. So, there is reciprocation: a positive flow of energy into the artifact and its life and a positive flow of energy from the artifact and its life. In such a process, the human beings who are using, interacting with, or living within the artifact have their own subtle lives and energy fields enriched. It's truly a win-win situation.

Unfortunately, for the most part and in most places, we are not living in such an ideal world in which everything is functioning with wholeness and integration as it should.

However, the challenge is that human imagination and purpose is often at odds both with our deeper soul wisdom and principles—and thus at odds with its artisanal spirit and potentials—and with the natural world around us and with the holistic efforts of the Devas and nature spirits that fill and bless that world. At this stage in our collective evolution, the human world of creativity and building becomes turned inward to our own benefit and purposes. We become disconnected from Gaia. When this happens, the subtle life within or associated with our artifacts becomes similarly disconnected as it is surrounded, enclosed, and shaped by humanity's collective energy. The bridge between humanity and nature becomes broken and, as we have seen in previous Field Notes, the techno-elementals become a breed apart, aligned more with humanity than with nature or with Gaia as a whole. Now we have this situation:

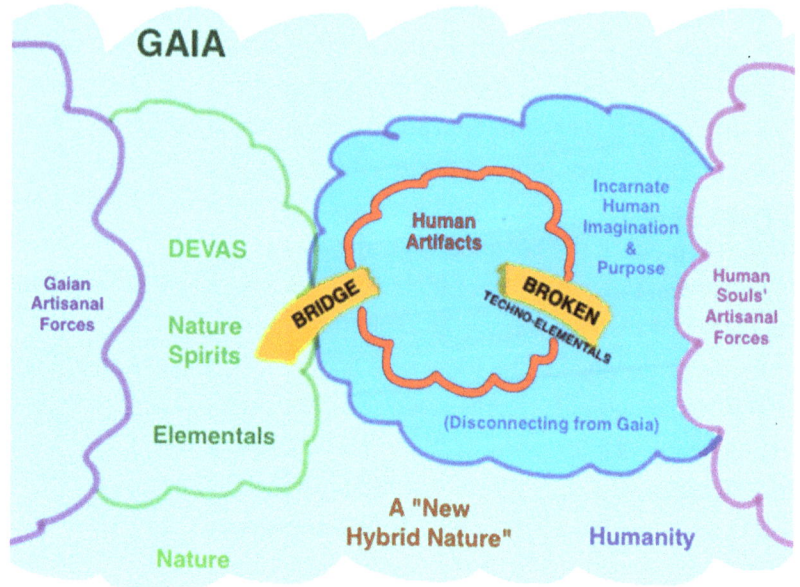

FIGURE 7
The Broken Bridge

This situation is complex. The disconnection between humanity and the rest of the world can manifest in many different ways energetically. For that matter, in some parts of the world where the connections between human beings and nature remain strong, the "bridge" may not be broken at all; in such places, techno-elementals may continue in good connection and flow with spiritual sources. But in much of our modern society, this is not the case.

This can create different problems for us and for the techno-elemental life that fills our built world, but there are four consequences of which I am most aware. There may well be others, but it's these four I want to focus on in these Field Notes. I think of them as **Internal, Environmental, Incarnational**, and **Evolutionary.**

The first problem is internal to the artifactals and to the techno-elemental kingdom as a whole. It is a dimming of the vitality, the energy, and the Light within the functions of the subtle organism.

This dimming creates an effect in the surrounding subtle

environment. This effect will impact the techno-elementals that are present but it can also impact the humans who are sharing that environment. It also increases the likelihood of psychic pollution and energetically stagnant conditions that can make possible the existence of negative forces I think of as "dark riders."

The lack of connection between the techno-elementals, particularly the artifactals, and the larger spiritual world can create a feedback loop that turns our creative energy, particularly will, back upon us to create a form of echo chamber. This can impact our incarnational activity, subverting our Sovereignty in unconscious ways. In a peculiar way, we create the artifact and then it shapes us.

Finally, our sense of what it means to be human can be narrowed and shaped by our technology, impacting our collective evolution. We can find ourselves living out as a species the ancient legend of the Golem, a creation of human beings that then turns and becomes a threat to its creators.

Techno-elementals and their subtle energies are involved in all four of these impacts upon us. Understanding how this happens gives us insights into what we can do to avoid these consequences and restore wholeness to ourselves, our artifacts, and our world.

FIELD NOTE 15: DIMMING

Between 2000 and 2010, I had a series of surgeries for recurring bladder cancer. Most of these operations took place in a hospital about twenty miles north of where I live. Then a new hospital opened up in my town and, finding the closeness to home more convenient, subsequent surgeries took place there.

Hospitals are themselves artifacts, made up, of course, of a great many other things, medical and otherwise, that humans design and manufacture. One could say they are an "artifactal ecosystem." This whole ecosystem is encompassed by a techno-elemental being who embodies the integrative identity and purpose of the building, giving it energetic coherency. At the same time, a hospital is overlighted by one or more angels of healing, who act as the allies or the sacramental for the building. I have not, fortunately, been in a great many hospitals throughout my life, but every time I have entered one, I've been aware of these great angelic beings.

The first hospital I was in for bladder surgery was relatively old and well-established; I was delighted to find as I lay in my room both before and after the operation that the flow of healing energies throughout the building was very strong. The walls themselves seemed to radiate with this force. When I tried, as I do in many buildings I enter, to reach out to the techno-elemental lives within the walls in acknowledgement and blessing, they immediately responded with appreciation and a reciprocal blessing. I had the sense that the techno-elemental of the hospital as a whole was very connected both to the land around it and to the larger spiritual worlds. It was energetically alive, and I felt myself lovingly held by the subtle environment it generated. An energy of service seemed baked into its bones.

This hospital was in an area that was a combination of shops and medical offices, not at all a rural or country setting. The second, newer hospital, by contrast, was built in the forested foothills surrounding the valley where I live, a beautiful natural setting. If any building was going to be connected energetically to the landscape around it, this one would have been a good candidate. However, the first three times I went there for surgery, it was energetically dead. The techno-elementals I felt within the walls were diminished in presence. I could feel a healing angel overlighting the place, but its influence and energy only penetrated so far into the hospital itself. It was a like a distant presence, hovering but not landing. I could feel the presence of numerous nature beings associated with the surrounding forests and mountainside, but I could feel a gap between the hospital and them. The difference in energy between this hospital and the previous one was dramatic to me.

I want to be clear that I'm speaking here of the subtle energies I felt in the structures themselves, the walls, the floors, the ceilings, and so forth. It has nothing to do with the personnel. Both hospitals are filled with kind, compassionate, dedicated, loving people seeking to serve the ill and injured who come there. These doctors, nurses, orderlies, and technicians create the human atmosphere of healing and care within the building. But they and the patients are enclosed in a structure that is itself a manifestation of living energy, and the quality of that energy does make a difference.

To be fair, I had my first surgery in this new hospital only a few months after it opened. The staff, the doctors, the nurses were all excellent and caring, but the place itself was new. Energetically, it was still finding its feet, so to speak. Over the years as I've gone there for more operations, I've felt it become more energetically alive, though from my perspective it is still not at the level of the first hospital I attended. Still, good changes are occurring in the subtle environment of the place as it has settled in.

There is one important difference between the two hospitals. The first hospital was designed by people who wanted to create a temple of healing. I have no idea if the original architects and builders had any knowledge of the subtle realms, but I was told by a doctor who had served in that hospital for years that, though it was a secular enterprise, the founders had been inspired to create a place that was as dedicated to spirit and spiritual healing as it was to medicine and physical healing. The second hospital on the other hand, the one near my home, has come under criticism for being "too commercial." The main floor looks less like a hospital and more like a beautifully designed mall with a restaurant and shops. I have no doubt that those responsible for its design and construction wanted it to be a place of healing as well, but it doesn't have the same spiritual vibration as the hospital to which I first went. The doctors and nurses definitely embody a spirit of service, but I haven't felt that same spirit "baked into the walls" from the beginning. You do get a sense when you walk through the main floor of the hospital that the administration would like you to do some shopping!

Obviously, these are personal observations, and the comparisons between the two buildings aren't entirely fair. It's like comparing a seasoned, experienced doctor with an intern seeing her very first patient. Who knows what I might have felt had I gone to the first hospital when it opened in the early 1970s? It might have felt energetically dead as well.

What is going on here? How do these differences come about? This is a complex topic which takes us into exploring the nature and expression of subtle energies as a manifestation of life. It's beyond the scope of this book (though if you wish to investigate this further, you could start with my book, *Working with Subtle Energies*). However, I think I can simplify things, as long as we realize this is an oversimplification.

Look at Figure 8.

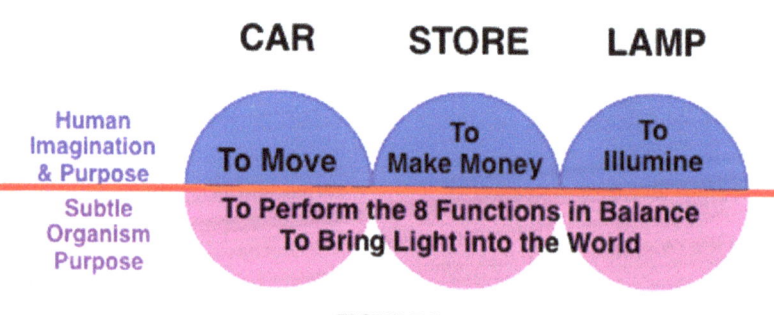

FIGURE 8
Different Purposes

Here are three different artifacts, a car, a store, and a lamp. These are very different items. The lamp is a single object, but the car is a more complex mechanism containing many parts, each of which is an artifact within the context of our discussions here. The store, on the other hand, is a building designed to house a commercial activity. It, too, is a complex artifact. Both the car and the store are "subtle ecosystems" comprised of a variety of techno-elementals, elementals of substance, potential riders, allies, and so forth. But each has a techno-elemental that represents the whole thing and holds the overall subtle ecosystem together as a coherent field of life and purpose.

Generally speaking for our simplified requirements, the purpose of the subtle organism is to express its eight basic functions, bringing Light into the world as it does so. It wishes to be, to become, and in the process, to express its inherent sacredness by contributing to wholeness in the world.

The human purposes, however, are different. They are very specific and usually reflective of personality desires and wishes. A human purpose for the car is to move, to provide transportation; there probably also is a commercial interest as well since car manufacturers aren't making their products to give away or to display as art objects in a museum! Similarly, the purpose of the store is to make money. If it fails to do so, whatever other purposes it may have, it will go out of business. And the purpose of the lamp is to illumine.

On a subtle level, human purposes are manifested as mental, emotional, and spiritual energies. This is not so different from the way my voice on a smartphone is turned into electrical impulses and my fingers moving across the keyboard of my computer are translated into a machine language that my computer can understand in order to produce the words on my monitor. When I hold the imagination to "make money" by constructing a building for a store, the etheric, subtle energy of this purpose becomes part of the subtle field of the structure as much as brick and mortar. It infuses the techno-elementals that form the subtle life of the building.

I do not expect, nor do I experience, the techno-elemental I sense in my desk lamp to exhibit a universal consciousness. It is focused upon being what it is and performing the function for which it was created as an artifact. Nevertheless, as a subtle lifeform, its natural state is to reach out to connect with the life around it. To the extent it is able, it will form connections to contribute to the unfoldment of wholeness in the environment around it. This is part of its purpose as well.

But human thought and intention are powerful in the subtle environment. They can easily shape the patterns and directions of subtle energies in and around an artifact, limiting the natural outflow and connectedness of the techno-elemental to the boundaries set by that intention. Rather than a partnership between the two intentions, that of the human and that of the subtle organism, the former overrides the latter. The challenge arises because so much of human imagination and intent is focused purely upon human needs and concerns and is not connective to a larger whole. Going back to the relationships and functions pictured in Figure 6 in the previous Field Note, we now have something like this:

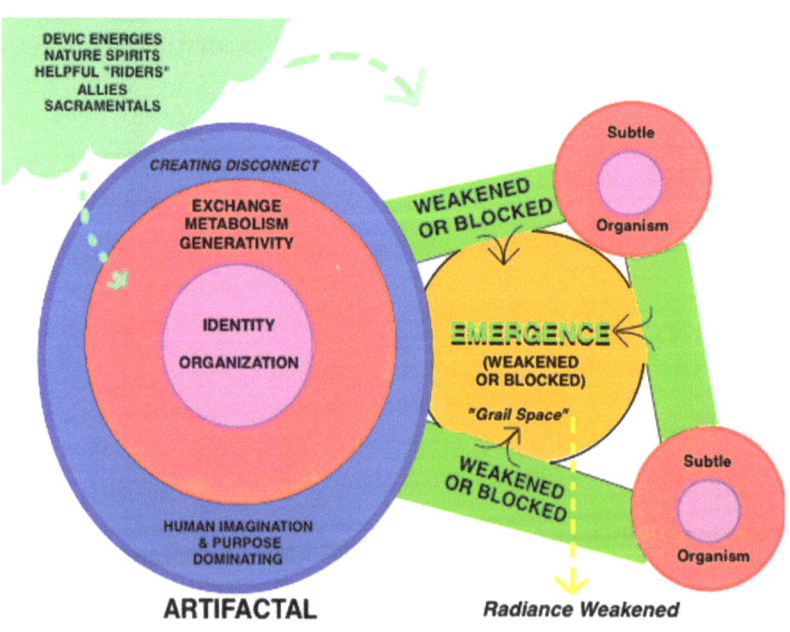

FIGURE 9
A Blocked Artifactal

Now the human energy of our purpose and imagination is acting as a barrier to connection with the larger spiritual and subtle worlds. This weakens or even blocks the natural flow of enlivening and supportive energies from those worlds into the life-systems of the techno-elementals, particularly the artifactals, associated with that artifact.

In the process, all the functions of the subtle organism are diminished. Its generativity is reduced, its metabolism is slowed down, its power to connect with other subtle organisms, techno-elementals, nature spirits, and on, particularly in holopoietic ways, is weakened or blocked, and its ability to create or co-create Grail Space and thus to evolve is similarly weakened or blocked.

To put it simply, the Light within this subtle life is dimmed, its radiance diminished. Its innate capacity to participate in Gaia's life is likewise diminished. The result is that the life within our built environments and the capacity of these environments and the things in them to support our own subtle well-being, is also reduced.

As I said, this is a complex topic for, like any ecosystem, the interplay and interactions between humanity and the subtle organisms that comprise both the natural and the humanly-built worlds are many and varied. Take my two hospitals, for instance. Each is a building containing hundreds of thousands of artifacts. Among these, many will be "dimmed" and many will be radiant, depending on what went into their manufacture but even more importantly the relationship that human beings have with them. For as we will see, the simple act of loving and appreciating an object can act like a breath of air upon an ember, causing it to reignite into a flame.

When I write about these hospitals as "artifacts," I am speaking generally of them as structures which, apart from all that they contain, have their own energetic radiance. Both hospitals were created to be places of healing and both hospitals were created as businesses needing to generate income to survive. However, in the case of the first hospital, the dominant human purpose was to make a "temple of healing" and in the case of the second, it was commercial success. The difference in emphasis shows up in the energy fields of the hospitals. Even today, for all that it has improved, the subtle presence of the newer, second hospital seems to me still not as energetically connected and integrated with its natural environment, in spite of the vitality and beauty of that environment itself, as the first hospital is with its surroundings, even though it is mainly in a commercial district of its town.

Whatever the impact of human thought and emotion upon them, subtle organisms cannot die. Their Light and life cannot be extinguished. However, they can be "dimmed" to a point of dormancy or inertness in which they become obstructions to the flow of subtle energies. The consequences of this are the subject of the next Field Note.

FIELD NOTE 16: SOOT

A twenty-minute drive from my house brings me to one of the natural wonders of our area, Snoqualmie Falls, where the Snoqualmie River plunges 268 feet over a cliff as it makes its way to Puget Sound. This site has long been considered sacred by the local Native American tribes, and it's not difficult to see why. Even without any sensitivity to the subtle energies of the place, the setting itself is beautiful and inspiring.

In 1916, a lodge was built on the rise overlooking the Falls. Since then, it has expanded into a large, luxury resort with an adjoining park where families can picnic and enjoy the setting and the view and even hike a trail down the cliff to the river below. It was often a favorite place to take our children when they were young.

There is another trail that leads to the Falls. This one approaches from the lower Snoqualmie River and is a long hike through rough, forested terrain. Eventually, you come out at the bottom of the Falls, across the river from the trail descending down the cliff from the lodge.

One day, we decided to visit the Falls using this trail. As we were hiking along, I suddenly entered into an altered state of awareness and found myself seeing everything around me from the perspective of one of the nature spirits of the forest. It was an awesome moment. I've never taken psychedelic drugs of any kind, but I could imagine it was the kind of thing a person "on a trip" might experience. I found myself in the midst of a riot of conversations going on between the bushes, the trees, the shrubs, the stones, the soil, everything around me, a conversation conducted in bursts and currents of color, energy, and what seemed to me to be a constant exchange of molecules. I remember thinking, "It's all chemistry! Everything is chemistry!"

This state lasted maybe five minutes or so as I walked along. I could feel and at times see the small nature spirits active within the forest and felt myself held within the energy field of a larger being, whose perspective I seemed to be sharing.

All at once, we topped a rise, and before me, though a clearing in the branches, I could see the Falls ahead of us and the lodge sitting next to them. To my surprise, instead of a beautiful building—and the lodge *is* beautiful—I saw something dark and unpleasant. For all the activity of the humans in and around the lodge, who generated their own kind of lively subtle energy, to the nature spirit whose consciousness I was temporarily sharing, the building was energetically dead, creating a zone that seemed to obstruct the flow of subtle life around it. It was like seeing a patch of dead skin on an otherwise healthy animal.

Around it, I sensed a turbulence of force in the subtle environment, like water rushing around a boulder placed into a river. It felt as if currents of energy were being blocked or diverted in some manner that I couldn't fully perceive or understand. Yet, I could feel the disharmony that was the result. Something akin to what in Britain is called a *ley line* was being compromised.

The thought and energy that goes into the lodge is largely commercial—it's a spa and resort, after all, and an expensive one! Creating energetic harmony and connection with the surrounding environment was probably not the uppermost thought in its construction. The result, at least as far as the nature spirit who showed me this was concerned, is a subtle form that acts as an obstruction rather than a partner to the subtle energies of the land. It doesn't heighten the beneficial effects of the ley line as much as it diminishes them.

In an ideal situation, life-supporting, life-nourishing, and life-empowering subtle energies flowing through the subtle environments of the world would flow in an unobstructed manner through the domains of nature, humanity, and our artifacts, as the sketch following indicates.

ARTFACTS
FIGURE 10
Unobstructed Flow of Gaian Life-Energies

This flow of life-force contributes to the overall health and wholeness of the planetary system and its interrelated subtle and physical ecosystems. If this flow is obstructed, then any subtle organisms affected by that obstruction may well experience less life-energy to work with and less stimulation for their own evolution. Their ability to participate in the collective function of emergence as represented by Grail Space may be diminished, as I have discussed.

I want to go back to the experience I recounted in Field Note 3. You will remember that I was alerted by a nature spirit to observe a ribbon of golden Light descending upon the neighborhood, or at least that is how my mind and inner vision interpreted what was happening. This was not the first or only time I've been aware of this phenomenon. As I said, I'm aware of currents of blessing radiating out from the great Deva overlighting Mt. Rainier to the south of where I live and from other similar Devas overlighting the mountains that surround the Puget Sound area. Likewise, on a smaller scale, I'm aware at times of Light radiating into the neighborhood from the being I call the Lady of the Lake overlighting Lake Sammamish. There is nothing unusual about this; such currents or emanations of life-force and blessing from higher-frequency beings is a vital part of subtle ecosystems everywhere.

Subtle energy outpourings and blessings like the golden ribbon I saw descending like mist onto my neighborhood are eventually absorbed by the elementals, nature spirits, and other subtle beings and spirits, enhancing both the non-physical and physical life of the area. However, it is not absorbed equally. The soil, the plants, the trees, and I imagine, the animals that make up the neighborhood seemed to take it in easily. But cars, houses, light posts, and other artifacts not so much. It depended on the vitality and connectedness of the techno-elementals associated with those artifacts. Some were very responsive, others—as far as I could tell—not so much.

Over the years, as I've walked through my neighborhood, I have noticed that some houses are surrounded and filled with a vital energy field while others are less so, and a few seem to have no energetic life to speak of, even though they are not empty but are homes to families. A diminished house-field doesn't necessarily tell me anything about the occupants of the house, only that the techno-elementals of that structure are largely ignored and are in what in a human being would be an unconscious or barely conscious state, a condition not at all unusual for artifacts in the modern world.

In the modern world, we are increasingly creating artifacts and environments that diminish or break the natural connections between the larger subtle environment and the techno-elementals, particularly the artifactals, often to their detriment. Rather than the unbroken flow we saw in Figure 10, now the situation looks like this:

FIGURE 11
Obstructed Flow of Gaian Life-Energies

It is as if the life-energy, the sentiency, within our artifacts becomes inert, which can act as a drag upon the whole of the subtle environment. When sensitives talk about how "dense" matter is, it is this condition surrounding and affecting the energy fields of our artifacts that they may be experiencing.

Again, I want to stress that not all artifacts and structures are disconnected from the flow of subtle energies. Our cities, towns, villages, and countrysides are filled with buildings that are both connected to and resonant with the subtle realms and those that are not, that act as boulders in a flowing stream.

It's way too simplistic to say that cities are disconnected simply because they are human artifacts. This is not a "city vs. nature" affair. It's quite possible for areas in nature to become energetically enclosed and disconnected as well. The main difference is that if and when this occurs in a non-human environment, there are subtle forces and beings—functioning a bit like a human immune system—that can respond to restore harmony, balance, and connectedness. In a human environment, this is less automatic and can be problematic since the constant barrage of human thought and emotion can make the work of such beings difficult. It's hard to clean a wall if someone is continually marking it up!

This is an environmental challenge, much as pollution is in the physical world. The problem is that we don't recognize the problem. We can be aware when a place doesn't "feel right" or has a "bad atmosphere," but in our materialistic society, we generally don't grasp how deep or extensive an effect this can be. We don't recognize the impact of subtle energies nor how that impact can affect our bodies and our minds and emotions. Equally, we don't recognize how our own thinking and feeling can affect the subtle environment around us. We know how our minds and emotions affect our bodies and vice versa. The links between our psychology and our physiology are well-explored. Similarly, many people have an understanding and an experience of how the spiritual dimension affects their lives. What we lack is a comparable understanding of how we are affected by what happens in the subtle environment around us. If the energy-life of our artifacts and the artifactals within them is diminished, our subtle life can be diminished as well. We are deprived of whatever Light they might ordinarily give us, but even more, we are cut off from the vitalizing flows of subtle energies and life-force from the spiritual realms of nature. Living in the midst of human-generated energy fields, we end up stewing in our own psychic juices.

An example of what I mean occurred when I was invited to do a workshop at a spiritual conference center in the early Eighties. When I began my workshop, I felt like I was having to "push through" a fog. I could sense the participants feeling uneasy and even irritable in ways that had nothing to do with anything I was saying.

During a break, I used my inner perception to examine the room (something I should have done right off the bat), and discovered that the walls were covered with "psychic grime." It was evident that this was the cause of the unpleasant feelings in the room. I asked one of the people running the center what the room was used for, and she said that it was where they regularly held Primal Scream and other types of psychologically cathartic workshops. In effect, people were regularly dumping their negative emotions and thoughts into the subtle environment of the room where it was being soaked up like psychic lint and soot by the walls and ceiling and floor. This had been going on for months, and during this time, no one was doing any kind of energy hygiene or cleansing in the room after all the emotional discharging was finished.

I called on my own subtle allies and the spiritual allies of the center itself and did an energy cleansing during the lunch break. That took care of the problem, and the workshop continued in a refreshed and vitalized atmosphere that everyone could feel and appreciate.

This was a mild case of energetic soot caused by techno-elementals being unable to refresh and recharge themselves. The conference center in question was run by dedicated people whose intent to serve people psychologically and spiritually brought its own Light into the place that helped compensate. However, in places where human suffering and violence are the norm, especially over time as a result of intent, and where hatred, fear, and other negative emotions have been prevalent, a subtle energy environment can be created that invites and sustains truly malicious and hurtful "dark riders." They become insulated from the Light by the disconnectedness of the artifactals within the structure or within the artifacts used to create harm.

Such dark riders can be anything from human-generated thought-forms to subtle lifeforms broken and damaged in themselves. They can exert a negative and malevolent influence on the subtle environments and the minds and emotions of those who participate in such environments or who use artifacts corrupted in this manner. Cleansing such a situation requires special resources and skills, a deep capacity for love and for equanimity and peace, and an unshakable attunement to the Sacred. Like cleaning up a toxic waste dump on the physical, it is something that requires knowledge, training, and the right equipment. It's not something to be tackled in a casual or unprepared way.

Fortunately, most of our environments, at least in my experience, do not attract nor can they sustain such truly negative and evil dark riders. But unless efforts are made to keep our energetic subtle environments clean and the techno-elementals blessed and aligned—something I will discuss in more detail in a later Field Note—any environment can accumulate a layer of energetic soot. When this happens, negative emanations born of our own emotions and thoughts can linger and be an influence upon us longer than they might be otherwise. Our own subtle energy resources can be diminished in response.

The disconnection and diminishment of vitality and Light I have been describing primarily affects the artifactals and, as I pointed out, the kind of "riders" that may attach to them. Other types of allies and Sacramentals are less affected in themselves, but the diminished energetic conditions can make it more difficult for them to connect and align with a given artifact, whether it's an object like my chalice or a structure like a building. They may wish to help but find it energetically difficult to do so. I may invoke a higher-frequency spiritual being, such as an angel, to overlight a particular object like my chalice, but if I have not cleansed its energy field and awakened its own inherent sentiency and life, the invocation may not "stick." No talisman is created, nor is any Sacramental or ally aligned, though I might pretend that these things have happened simply because I did an invocation or ritual.

FIELD NOTE 17: ECHOES

I was visiting a close friend for the first time in his own home. We'd known each other for years, but I'd never had the opportunity before to travel to the State where he lived. He and his wife lived in a large home, and he was proudly showing me around when he took me into the master bedroom. "I want to show you something," he said.

He went over to a small table near his bed and, opening the drawer, took out a large revolver. "We've been having break-ins in the neighborhood," he said, showing me the gun. "So, I got this. It's a Magnum revolver, and believe me, I know how to use it!"

He then handed me the weapon. Unlike my friend, who had grown up in a gun-culture, guns had never been a part of my life. So, this was the first time I'd ever held a revolver. I was curious about it, so as I held it, I tuned in to the techno-elemental life within it. I'm not sure what I was expecting, but what I found surprised me and gave me a deeper look at the role of techno-elementals in our lives.

I discovered myself in contact with a presence that was proud of what it was as a gun and that wanted to be used for the purposes for which it had been created. This was in no way an evil or negative entity (which is not to say a "dark rider" couldn't attach itself to a weapon) but merely a subtle organism—I believe of an elemental nature, though it's not always easy for me to discern the exact "species" involved—that had taken on the human purpose for which this artifact had been produced and, like a good servant, was intent on following it out. It was designed to kill, and it was prepared to do so. It wanted to fulfill its function.

There was no ill-will present in this being, and it certainly had no target in mind. It didn't have the kind of consciousness that would give it any sense of morality. The gun wasn't possessed, as in some horror story, by a disembodied entity that was looking for victims. It was simply an impersonal, one might even say blind, devotion to the human purposes instilled in it through its design and creation. In this sense, the nearest analog might be a robot seeking to fulfill its programming.

I realized holding this revolver that if there were anything in me that would resonate emotionally or mentally to this embodied purpose, that is, if I were trying to decide whether to kill someone or not, the subtle energy held in the techno-elemental of this weapon could act as an echo chamber, magnifying and playing back to me my own intent to do harm. The gun's desire to fulfill its purpose and my desire to shoot someone could combine to tip me over from merely thinking about killing to actually doing so.

Before we begin blaming the techno-elementals of weapons for all the mayhem and violence in our world, I want to be clear that this is a complex issue. Why a person commits an act is a child with many parents. There are psychological reasons, karmic reasons, social reasons, environmental reasons. We all have sovereignty and choice, and we are the agents who make decisions to harm or not to harm. But as I've been saying throughout this book, we are also subtle beings operating in a subtle environment. Subtle energies do have an effect upon us psychologically and physiologically. This is why being aware of techno-elementals is important because they are an influence in our lives. At any given time in any given circumstance, this influence could be minor or it could be major; it could be beneficial, or it could be harmful. But whatever it may be, it is always there as long as we live within and surrounded by our artifacts.

I thought, holding this gun and feeling its dedication to its purpose, that if a person were emotionally and mentally at a tipping point, the nudge of this techno-elemental energy might be one of the factors sending him or her over the edge into violence.

Then I felt something else with this revolver. In addition to the basic will to fulfill its purpose—in effect, to be useful and to be used—there was another layer of energy which, I realized, came from my friend. It was like seeing a second set of instructions added on to the original programming. It's hard to put this into words, but the image that arose in my mind was that of a guardian. This is anthropomorphizing, I realize, but the closest I can come to what I was feeling was that the gun saw itself as a protector. It was clear that this energetic attitude had been added, rather like energy is added to a talisman, after the gun had been designed and manufactured, and it was clear it reflected my friend's attitude and overall energy field. Although raised around and with guns, he was a very loving and gentle man. If pushed, he would push back, and he was fearless in doing so, but he was not a violent personality. He did have, however, especially where his family and people he loved were concerned, a strong commitment to being a protector.

He had purchased the gun to protect his family and household. This intent was strong enough and held often enough when he thought of the gun to communicate to the techno-elemental of the revolver, altering its sense of purpose from "killing" to "killing to protect."

I realize my words can make it sound as if the gun, or more precisely, the techno-elemental, has agency in the human sense, but it does not. It *is* a "thou," but it's not a person. Its consciousness is not structured or capable in any way that would express human capacities. But it does possess an awareness of itself and a desire to fulfill its reason for being.

Since that experience, I've explored this phenomenon more deeply and have decided, barring further information and insights, that what I was tuning into with my friend's gun was an extension of the artifactal energy and consciousness into what I think of as a "rider of purpose." I want to make clear that trying to draw distinctions between different layers of energy and identity with entities whose boundaries are more fluid than anything we experience in the physical world, is not easy and subject to error. It's like trying to focus a microscope to see the fine differences within the body of a cell and, if the instrument doesn't focus that well, you end up seeing blurry images. You can make deductions from these images, but they can be mistaken.

As I've discussed in previous Field Notes, the energy and thought-forms of human imagination and purpose can enter and shape the characteristics of artifactals. If the human producing that energy and those thought-images is not particularly connected to the larger wholeness of the world, then the human contribution creates a diminished state. Since human thought is powerful, this diminished state can end up being the dominant characteristic of the artifactal and of other techno-elemental elements associated with it.

In this case, a "rider" is created that focuses upon fulfilling the purpose of the artifact. It is what I think of as a "vector of will," that is, an energetic projection of a will for something to happen. By itself, it may be small and weak, but in a collective setting, it can become much more powerful.

Thus, if, when building the walls of a hospital, the people involved project into the materials going into the walls an intent that they hold a healing energy, then a very powerful "vector of will" or "rider of purpose" comes into being as part of the techno-elemental energy of the hospital's physical structure. Of course, in today's materialistic world, it is probably rare that this happens, but in the future, when, hopefully, we have a greater awareness as a society of the reality and character of the subtle ecosystem around us and of which we are a part, then the holding and projection of appropriate thought-forms and mental energies as part of the construction process may become part of a builder's training. It can certainly happen now when a person builds his or her own home and puts their loving energy into every part of it.

The "rider of purpose" or the "vector of will" in my friend's gun was very simple: "Kill!" This is the fundamental purpose of the weapon as imagined, designed, and built by human beings. It's not a tool of building, of healing, of exploration. It is a tool of killing. However, this "rider of purpose" that I attuned to as part of the techno-elemental field—a rider created by human thought rather than a subtle entity in its own right come from some other part of the subtle worlds—was a small projection of energy. It was a small "vector of will." Any normal person holding the gun would be able to resist it, experiencing it, perhaps, simply as a stimulation to the imagination, wondering what it might be like to actually use the gun as it's intended to be used.

However, the power of guns and using them to kill is a powerful thoughtform within the collective imagination of humanity. Guns have been used for killing for hundreds of years, and they occupy a major part of both popular entertainment and the news of world events.

Guns are being used all around the world to kill, and thousands of people are dying daily because of their use.

Even leaving out any number of other factors—psychological, subtle, environmental, social, and so forth—that might lead a person to use a gun, the link of this powerful collective imagination and purpose within humanity with the tiny "rider of purpose" within a particular gun can give the latter much more power and influence than it might have otherwise. More precisely, the "rider of purpose" within the techno-elemental presence of the gun acts as a portal into the very much more powerful and influential energy and will of the thought-forms of gun use and killing held in the collective psyche of humanity. These are subtle energies—what I call "vectors" in that they embody momentum and direction translated into purpose—that want to be fulfilled. They "ground themselves" in the lives and actions of people who are susceptible.

This is a complex topic beyond the scope of this book. My point here is just that techno-elementals become places where human purposes and imaginations and desires can become anchored; our artifacts can hold these humanly-created energies the way a battery holds an energy until it is discharged.

In my own experience, most of our artifacts possess these "riders of purpose," but in most cases, they are relatively weak and without much consequence. For instance, my little Yoda figure, as I described earlier, has links to the collective image of Yoda. Part of its purpose is to represent this image. But it also has a "rider of purpose" which is commercial in nature. It is designed to be sold; at one level, it doesn't matter what it looks like as long as it is attractive to a buyer. As I have held and used this Yoda figure as an icon that for me represents a level of wisdom and attunement, the energy I've projected into it long ago "overwrote" and replaced that original "buy me" rider of purpose.

Some of the artifacts we create, like guns, have strong "riders of purpose," configurations of energy and intent that we create and project into their subtle energy field, shaping the artifactal accordingly; others are much weaker or even neutral. Most of these "riders of purpose" have little to do with fostering partnership with the subtle and physical life around us or with creating wholeness within the spiritual, subtle, psychological, and physical worlds we inhabit. They do not have a purpose of contributing in some manner to Gaia's well-being, or even to humanity's overall health and wholeness.

Therein lies a problem. We create and then live in an energetic echo-chamber based in our technology that reflects back to us who we are in our separateness as human beings but not who we are in our connectedness and wholeness with Gaia. We are encased in worlds of human imagination and purpose, which are powerful but not sufficient to reflect the fullness of who we are as sacred individuals.

Technology as a whole is like a collective techno-elemental of our own creation and invocation. We may question what kinds of technology we create or how we use technology, but we don't question the existence of technology itself. We create more technology because we can or because there is a need for it, real or imagined, but contributing to this growth of the modern technological world is the subtle energy of technology as a thing in itself, a planetary "artifact" in itself. It is a collective "rider of purpose," influencing us as a species and energizing and stimulating our own desire to create more technology. It has the power to shape our evolution.

FIELD NOTE 18: SHAZAM!

I have always been a fan of superheroes. As a kid, I reveled in the adventures of Superman as chronicled in various D.C. comic books. However, my loyalties were severely tested when I discovered a rival comic book company, Fawcett Comics, and their superhero, Captain Marvel. He had a variety of superpowers similar (and even identical) to those of Superman (which later led to charges of copyright violation by the creators of the Man of Steel), but there was one major difference. Superman came from another planet. I might admire him, but in my imagination, I couldn't really *be* him. I was from earth, he wasn't. Captain Marvel, on the other hand, was actually a boy my age, Billy Batson, who could transform into the superhero by uttering a magic word given him by an ancient wizard: Shazam! In the comics, he would be hit by a bolt of magic lightning when he said this, and suddenly, it wasn't Billy standing there anymore. It was Captain Marvel! Now *this*, my eight-year old mind decided, was within the realm of possibility, if only I could find the right ancient wizard….

In a way, humanity had its own "Shazam moment" and was struck with a transforming bolt of lightning when Benjamin Franklin flew his kite in a lightning storm, an iconic image of the start of our electronic technology. We even had an iconic wizard, Thomas Edison, often referred to as the "Wizard of Menlo Park" for all the wonders and discoveries he produced from his laboratory in New Jersey, U.S.A.

Humanity may not have become a superhero but we definitely gained superpowers through the mastery of electromagnetism. The flow of electricity is the lifeblood for our modern civilization, a civilization that has radically transformed the planet in ways that were never possible for humanity before.

It also brought us into association with a new domain of elemental and spiritual energies and consciousnesses, as I described in Field Note 12. These beings are not the same kind of techno-elemental as those I've been describing, such as the artifactals and the riders. Nor are they exactly allies. Yet, they definitely come into contact and interaction with us through our technology and our tool-making. Though part of Gaia and Earth's evolution, they are a form of subtle life and consciousness with which we have not "grown up" over the millennia. This relative unfamiliarity presents a set of challenges different from those we have been exploring in previous Field Notes.

As I said in the earlier Field Note, electrical elementals are beings of force, closest in nature, I think, to elementals of fire, but at the same time, they are more fundamental. They are expressions of cosmic forces of manifestation itself; they help make the universe possible.

In relationship to us, they are not hybrids. They can associate with artifactals, but they are not elementals of substance. They are not tied to particular artifacts. They can augment human purposes but they don't blend with them in the way other techno-elementals do, at least as far as I can tell (and remember, this is an exploratory, investigative process for me, too!).

Thus, when I tune into the techno-elemental life of my desk lamp, I can perceive the artifactal and I can sense the presence of an electro-elemental or an "intelligence and spirit" of electricity, but the two are not the same. The electro-elemental is not, to my sensing, at least, a being—a distinct entity—in the way the artifactal of the lamp is, and yet it adds its power to that artifactal in order for it to fulfill its purpose. In effect, what I am perceiving here is a symbiotic relationship, analogous, I suppose, to lichen, which is a composite organism comprised of algae and fungi, two distinctly different forms of life.

The energetic influence of my lamp, such as it may be, is limited in scope. I may feel it while I'm sitting at my desk, but I don't feel it when I'm across the room or in another room. The energetic influence of electricity, however, is not so limited. The lamp in my bedroom on the other side of the house resonates with the same electro-elemental energy and influence as the lamp on my computer desk. The artifactals are different, but the electromagnetic presence is the same.

On the whole, my experience of the presence of electro-elemental life is that it manifests as a field rather than as a point source. I can point to where the artifactal of my lamp is, but the electro-elemental presence is really all around me in the house and in the neighborhood outside. Electrical wires are everywhere carrying current throughout my home and the homes around me. Radio waves, including the microwaves used for cell phone transmissions, fill the air around me, broadcast from local television and radio stations and from cell phone towers. Although electromagnetic waves of all kinds have always been in the world, our civilization is deliberately generating them and filling the spaces we live in with them in unprecedented ways. Unlike other techno-elementals that are in the environment *with* us, electro-elementals *surround* us. They *become* the environment in which we live. I suggest this in Figure 12.

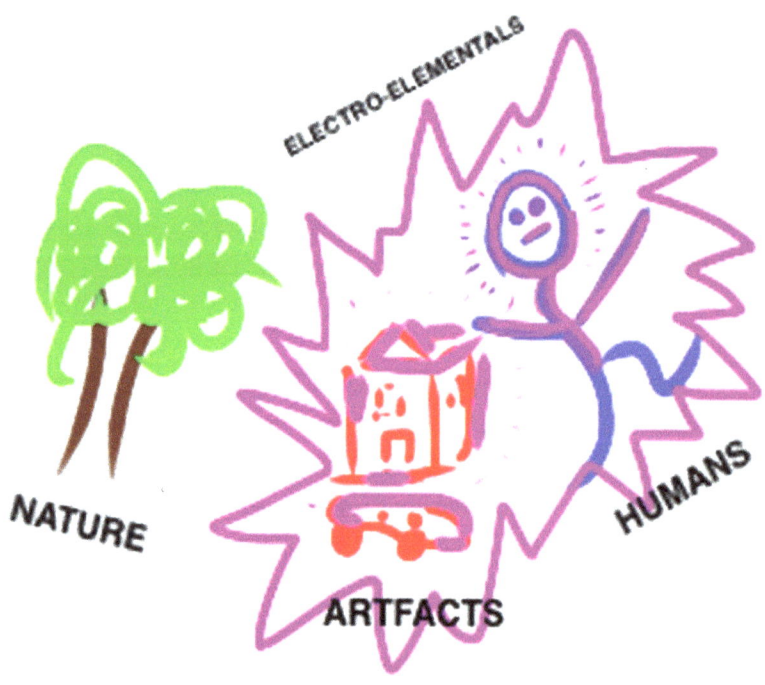

FIGURE 12
Humanity Encompassed by Electro-Elementals

This sets up a situation in which we adapt to the fields created by electro-elementals rather than the other way around. They become a ubiquitous influence in ways other techno-elementals do not.

What is this influence?

As I described in Field Note 12, when I first began investigating the nature and impact of electro-elementals as part of my larger techno-elemental research, I had a negative impression of them. All techno-elementals are non-human subtle organisms, even though we may project human-like qualities and characteristics upon them; but my experience of the electro-elementals was that they were *inhuman*. This inhumanity—which I perceived then as a cold, impersonal, inorganic force—was off-putting to me and even sinister. Electro-elementals seemed to me like something from an alien dimension whose effect upon us was deleterious, diverting us from our human evolutionary path. They seemed wholly devoid of love.

There is some truth to this perception, at least at a surface level, but it doesn't go deeply enough. It offers a good lesson in not stopping with first impressions, especially when dealing with subtle world phenomena whose nature is outside incarnate human experience. As I said in Field Note 12, I have subsequently discovered a loving, spiritual presence—what I might think of as the Devic presences overlighting electromagnetic energy. It has become clear to me that rather than being an alien intrusion into human evolution, the increasingly strong presence of electro-elementals in our lives has been directed by spiritual forces whose long-term interest is in the well-being and wholeness of humanity, as well as of the Earth. There are indeed love and warmth present in the electro-elemental realm, if one goes deeply enough to see it.

This doesn't mean, though, that this development of electrical technology doesn't have its risks and challenges. Electromagnetic phenomena can definitely have unhealthy effects on our physical bodies, some of which we are still discovering. But my interest in this book is on how it affects our subtle nature, at least as much as I am able to discern at this point.

There are two effects that stand out for me.

The first of these is the newness of this relationship. However much electromagnetism and electricity are part of the natural world, the manner in which we are living with these energies is an unprecedented product of human technology. As I have said, we have not evolved in close relationship and partnership with electro-elementals the way we have with other elemental and Devic beings. Therefore, we are getting to know each other. Our two evolutionary lines are having to explore how to interact in ways that augment and help each other rather than hindering or negatively impacting each other. The consciousness inherent in the subtle life of electricity does not perceive or respond to the world in the way a human consciousness does. The problem is that we are still discovering, as incarnate beings, just what it means to be human; we are learning who we are and what our capabilities are. The electro-elementals know very well what who they are and what they can do.

Like any elemental force, electro-elementals are very strong and clear in their identity and energy, and this strength and clarity can influence us unless we are equally clear and strong in our humanity. For instance, electricity "thinks" and operates in binary ways. Its consciousness is structured to express a simple but powerful logic of positive and negative poles, on and off. Human consciousness is more complex and flexible. We experience polarities and binaries in our lives, such as male and female, but we are not limited to them. We can express gender in multiple ways, not just two. We are capable of seeing "yes" and "no," but also "maybe" and "in addition." We operate in areas of ambiguity that are unknown to the elemental worlds generally and the electro-elementals specifically.

The challenge here is that, with the human world surrounded and pervaded by the elemental influence of electricity, we can become less human. Our humanity takes on from the electro-elemental realm tendencies that constrict it in ways not suitable for the evolution of our consciousness. We do this in part because we are trying to adapt to a new kind of environment and in part because we would like to appropriate the power of electro-elementals for ourselves, and we think the way to do this is to become more like them.

This brings us to the second effect. The cosmic subtle force of which electromagnetism is an outward manifestation heightens the energy of other life processes. It can speed them up, which means that human evolution becomes accelerated—which we can see in the acceleration over the past century of human technology. This acceleration is not necessarily deeply rooted; it can be a surface phenomenon, like a young person who grows quickly into the body and strength of an adult while still at the emotional stage of a child.

The rage for efficiency in business that began in the first part of the Twentieth Century is an example of this. The factory assembly line greatly speeded up and increased production, but it turned individual persons into parts in an industrial machine. Another example that is more recent is the shrinkage of our power of attention. People want their information in short, digital bites—hence the popularity of texting and tweeting—and lose their willingness, if not their ability, to read in a deep, contemplative manner. The evening news gives a series of swift snapshots of the day's events, often concentrating on what is visually exciting, without a concomitant exploration and analysis of these events that would provide context and meaning.

The impact of the electro-elemental subtle field increasingly surrounding humanity isn't forcing us to be a certain way or to do certain things, but it emphasizes tendencies existing in our consciousnesses. It speeds up and intensifies our emotional and mental reactions, which can have both good and bad consequences depending on what these reactions are or the depth of consciousness they represent. The simplest effect is that it increases stress. Because of the speed of our electrical environment, it is harder, unless we are deliberate about it, to find moments and places of quiet and calm where our lives can slow down. The ubiquitousness of our smartphones means that we are never out of connection with others but it also means we are always being engaged by others when what we may need is to be left alone.

I've come to realize as I've pursued this research that the electro-elemental world truly wants to partner with us and in doing so, to be of positive benefit. But they don't understand us and, from their point of view, we don't understand ourselves very well. Because we can be fluid and pliable in our energy, they can influence us in ways they don't intend. Likewise, we don't understand them because we have such little understanding of the wholeness of life, especially in its subtle aspects. There is much for both sides to learn here. The challenge is whether we will rise to the occasion. Hit by the subtle lightning of the electro-elemental world, do we turn into a superhero for the Earth or are we merely incinerated?

FIELD NOTE 19: ROOMIES

Now we come to the most important question. How do we interact with techno-elementals in a way that benefits them and us? If techno-elementals are a "bridge" that is broken, how do we repair the bridge?

The techno-elemental challenge has two parts. One is environmental, and one is evolutionary. These subtle organisms live in and share humanly created environments; they are an integral part of the formation of these environments. They are the subtle life that intimately participates in our various artifacts, from the tools we use to the clothes we wear and the buildings we live in. A United Nations report issued in 2014 said that 54% of humanity now lived in cities; that percentage is undoubtedly larger now. If our ancestors lived in the midst of nature, most of us now live in midst of the things we have designed, fashioned, and manufactured. For many of us, artifacts *are* our daily, natural environment and techno-elementals often our equivalent of nature spirits.

Therefore, the nature of the environments we create directly affect techno-elementals who in turn affect the environments in which we live.

Like all organisms, subtle or physical, techno-elementals learn from and evolve within the environments in which they live. This means that humanity has a direct, though not an exclusive, impact on the evolutionary development of these beings. As I discussed in Field Note 4, we live in a learning universe. Techno-elementals learn by being part of human subtle energy fields of thought, emotion, and spirituality. They learn the way a singer learns a melody by hearing it repeated over and over again, or the way a muscle learns to throw a ball by throwing it over and over again. They learn by being part of or being influenced by how we perform the eight functions of a subtle organism. How do we, as more advanced beings, hold our identity? How do we exchange subtle energies? How do we process them? How do we form connections? How do we create wholeness in our environment—or fail to do so (it's possible to learn brokenness as well as wholeness)?

To imagine how we may positively affect techno-elementals environmentally and evolutionarily, think of two college roommates—a senior, let's say, and a freshman—sharing the same room in a dormitory. If the upperclassman clutters up the room and makes a mess, his roommate may have no option but to live in it; after all, freshmen don't tell seniors what to do! He may even learn to be messy, too, following by example. The upperclassman, being more experienced in the school, may not be too bothered by the mess, but the freshman may well find the environment distracting and not conducive to studying and learning.

It may seem evident that the senior needs to be aware of his mess, clean it up, and make a more learning-friendly environment for the freshman. But before he can do this, his first step is to look past their respective status in the college and recognize the freshman as a fellow student. Creating a better environment flows out of acknowledging and caring for the well-being of the freshman. It arises from a desire to make learning easier, not harder, for his roommate. After all, if both roommates are prospering, the environment they co-create will be beneficial for both

In dealing with techno-elementals, our first step, then, is recognizing they exist and honoring and appreciating their presence. We can't fix a broken bridge unless we see the bridge is there; we can't make a roommate comfortable unless we see that we *have* a roommate. This need not be a psychic experience. We don't have to wait until we're clairvoyant to acknowledge the subtle organisms and the subtle environment around us. A mental tip of the hat to their presence is a good place to start.

A large part of the challenge with techno-elementals is simply that we don't accept they exist. We don't accept the reality that everything around us—and I mean *everything*—is alive. We don't acknowledge that energetically and spiritually, we inhabit a world of subjects, not one of subjects and objects. Accepting and acknowledging that we are part of a living universe embracing both physical and non-physical realities is the needed first step. After all, the upperclassman can't create an environment more accommodating and helpful to the freshman sharing his room if he doesn't believe or acknowledge that the freshman exists.

Beyond recognizing the reality of the subtle realms and the existence of subtle organisms is acknowledging our impact upon those realms and beings through our own generative subtle nature. The very fact that he is in the same room as his roommate means the upperclassman is going to affect him. The messes he creates may be due to habits he's acquired when he thought he was living alone; continuing those habits will make it harder for his roommate. The senior now has to be mindful of the effect he is having. If he now chooses his actions and behavior out of respect and care for his roommate, he will help create a supportive environment for both of them.

We are constantly radiating through our thoughts and feelings and through our actions subtle and spiritual energies that impact the subtle environment around us and the beings inhabiting that environment. The more we turn these emanations into positive forces of blessing, love and appreciation for the life around us, the more we nurture the techno-elementals in our lives.

There is a tradition in many cultures of purifying an environment through the use of incense and fragrances. Smudging with a bundle of burning sage, for example, is common amongst many Native American tribes as a way of energetically cleansing a room.

From an inner standpoint, we are each surrounded with the "fragrance" of our incarnate nature, the expression of our spiritual, mental, emotional, and physical choices and activities. We are constantly "smudging" our immediate environment, impacting the techno-elementals around us with the "smoke" of our being, which may be uplifting and empowering or toxic and polluting. We are powerful forces of positivity or negativity, either organizing or disorganizing, cleansing or messing up the spaces our inner roommates must share with us.

If we understand this, then we are called to being a consistent loving presence in our world, something spiritual teachers have been asking of us for millennia! We are like living stars: we are always generating and radiating subtle energies that affect our world. The important thing is that we can affect and shape what we generate through our choices and our intentions. We have sovereignty and agency. This idea is at the core of Incarnational Spirituality. Our ability to choose and our ability to love are our primary tools in reconstructing the broken bridge of connection for the techno-elementals in our lives.

The simplest way to bless and energize our subtle environments—to "smudge" them with our love and appreciation—is through the ways we engage with their physical counterparts, that is, with the artifacts that make up our world. When I vacuum the living room, I can send love to the carpet and to the floor underneath it. When I do the dishes, I can be aware of loving each plate, each pan, each utensil. When I enter a room, I imagine my energy field expanding to fill the room with blessing and appreciation.

I don't need to be psychic or clairvoyant to do any of these things. I just need to appreciate how my thoughts and emotions shape my subtle energy field and how that field in turn impacts the energy fields of the subtle organisms around me. I don't even have to think about techno-elementals. All I need do is foster states of joy, of love, of vitality, of gratefulness within myself as an habitual way of being. This can't help but benefit my many "roommates."

What I have been describing is a relationship we have with techno-elementals that is automatic and largely unconscious. I do have to be conscious and mindful of the overall state of my subtle energy field—that is, of the quality of my thoughts and feelings—but I don't have to be aware of or thinking about the subtle environment and its inhabitants.

However, we can have a more focused relationship with the subtle world around us. We have the power through our attention and our intention to bring joy, love, gratefulness, and vitality to the techno-elementals that make up our subtle environment. We can intentionally energize any artifacts we use with acknowledgement, with appreciation, with love, and with any other positive quality we may wish and choose to share.

When I use an artifact, like, say, my coffee cup, I can take a moment to pay attention to it *as a living presence* and to direct thoughts and feelings of appreciation and love to it. When I see my desk lamp, I take a moment to appreciate and love it, too, *as a living presence*. When I put my fingers to the keyboard of my computer to write these words, I silently bless, honor, and love the keyboard that I'm touching.

If we do this consistently, it not only broadcasts a positive, life-affirming, energizing subtle energy to the artifacts to which we are giving our attention, it also begins to build in habits of thought and feeling that affect our energy fields overall. As I said above, we don't have to turn our attention to every artifact in our surroundings to give it appreciation and love; that would totally occupy our time to the exclusion of doing anything else! But we don't need to. If we're building habits of love and blessing into our subtle energy fields, then these qualities automatically radiate to positively affect our world.

It's the same principle as honoring people. If I am in a crowd of people, I don't need to go up to each one to say, "I appreciate you and love you for who you are!" If it's New Year's Eve on Times Square in New York City, the new year would be well advanced before I could say this to each individual who was there (assuming they waited there long enough for me to do so!). But if I have a loving, appreciative attitude in general, then this is what I will convey to whomever I meet—and on a subtle level, this creates a field of lovingness that touches and blesses many more than I could interact with physically.

A third thing we can do is to foster connectedness between our world of artifacts and the world of nature. There are different ways to do this. The simplest relies on the manner in which our personal subtle energy field engages with our surrounding environment. If we are attuned to nature and feel a connection with the natural world, this quality of attunement and connection manifests in our own energy fields and, as we have seen, can be passed on to any techno-elemental impacted or influenced by our field.

As I write this, my wife is taking advantage of a rare sunny day here in the Pacific Northwest to air out all the cushions and pillows from the sofas in the living room. Our back porch is covered with them, all basking in the rays of the sun. It looked so inviting that I took a "sun break" from writing to go out and join them. As I did so, I consciously invited blessing from the Air Devas upon all the techno-elementals in the pillows and cushions.

We can make a specific energetic connection between some part of nature and one or more artifacts. As another example, there is a large Douglas Fir tree that grows in our front yard close to the house. It is a dominant feature when looking through the front window of our living room. I can reach out to it, attuning to its life and energy field, and then ask it to project its blessings into the living room.

We can also attune to Devic presences and ask them to bless our artifacts and ensure their connection to the larger life-field of nature. For instance, sitting among the pillows and cushions while on my "sun break," I consciously invoked blessing from the Devas of the air to cleanse and vivify the artifactals within them. Likewise, I wrote earlier of the energy radiating from the being I call the "Lady of the Lake," a small Deva overlighting Lake Sammamish near where we live. I can attune to that presence and ask it to bless my house. Or I can—and often do—attune to the mountain Devas that surround the valley where I live, Mt. Rainier in particular, to do the same.

Another example is that when I used to travel by plane, I would attune to Air Devas. Then, as I I boarded the plane, I would greet the techno-elemental of the aircraft, offer it my blessings, and then use my attunement to offer it connection with the Devas of the air.

All of these are examples of ways I can improve the environment in which I find the techno-elementals around me. Doing so empowers their ability to be more connected and also, as a result, their ability to contribute positively to the overall subtle energies in which I live. When the upperclassman cleans up the room, the freshman is better able to settle in and contribute. The latter is also able to study better.

All of this falls under the broad heading of "energy hygiene." It is a way of cleansing and vitalizing our subtle environment. It is also a way to get rid of any undesirable "dark riders" or unwanted negative entities that may have been attracted or psychic pollution that may have accumulated. After all, if the upperclassman cleans up the room and helps the freshman do so as well, they are less likely to be infested with rats or other vermin.

The topic of subtle hygiene is larger than I can cover in this book. If you are interested in more detailed information, please see my book, *Working with Subtle Energies*.

We contribute to the evolution of techno-elementals by providing examples of how subtle energies may be positively embodied and expressed. If the senior in our dorm room has good study habits, the freshman is more likely to pick up on them and thus improve his own learning capacity.

However, techno-elementals are not on the human line of consciousness evolution. They are learning different life lessons, just like the freshman may be studying for a major in business administration while the upperclassman is studying to become an astrophysicist. Good study habits, so to speak, can be conveyed but not specific information. However, if the upperclassman creates a distracting, obstructive environment that keeps the freshman from studying properly, this is a problem.

This is what we do when we project a negative and disconnected subtle energy field into our environment, making it more difficult for the techno-elementals—particularly the artifactals—to learn what they need to learn and to connect with their "teachers," the higher expressions of Devic and Gaian life. From an evolutionary standpoint, we need to stop creating obstructions through the negativity we generate that diminishes techno-elemental vitality and life.

Beyond that, we can with practice and skill learn to attune to the angelic and Devic presences that overlight techno-elemental evolution. We can in our meditations and in our active blessings align with such presences and ask both that our human field not be an obstruction to their evolutionary work and that, where possible, it be a conduit for their blessing. We can ask that our lives assist and empower the natural evolutionary development of the subtle life within our artifacts.

I illustrate these different possibilities of positive engagement with techno-elementals in the picture following, Figure 13.

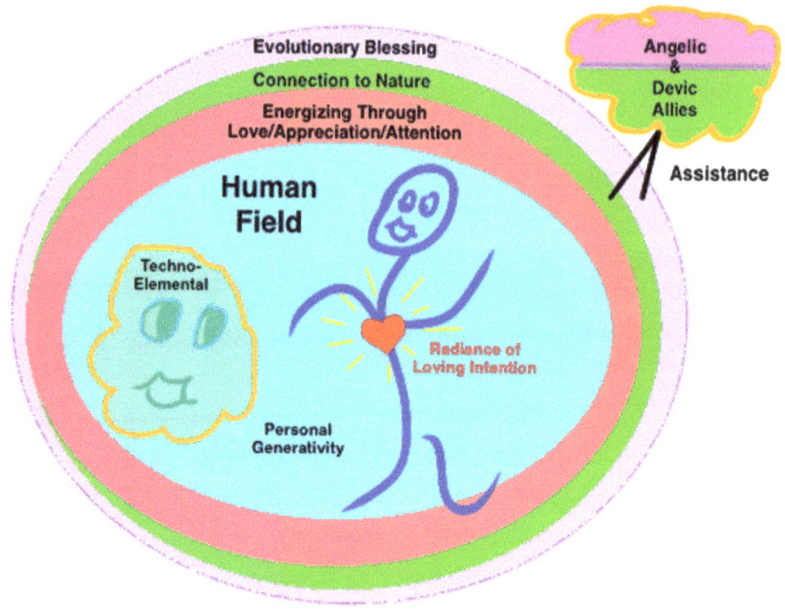

FIGURE 13
Engaging with Techno-Elementals

In Field Note 13, I discussed the collaborative, co-creative function of emergence, a key factor in the evolution of life and consciousness. I used the image of Grail Space as a way of imagining this function. With this in mind, one of the most important things we can do to assist the techno-elemental (and, for that matter, natural elemental) life around us is to use our internal ability to create Grail Space to do so externally. As I described in the earlier Field Note, human subtle energies can block artifactals from the connection with nature spirits that would ordinarily draw out and enhance their evolutionary potentials by co-creating Grail Space with them. Since we have drawn these beings into our world, we have a responsibility to provide this help, and we can do so using our own capacity to form Grail Space.

Using intention and love, we can reach out to the life and Light within the subtle organisms in our environment, inviting them to join us and participate in jointly bringing a Grail Space into being. Such a space creates a field that empowers and heightens the evolutionary processes of all who take part. We are sharing our Grail Space-making capacity with those subtle lives who normally cannot do so on their own.

In the Appendix, I offer a suggested exercise in creating Grail Space.

Mostly, we want to remember that the lives within the artifacts that surround us in our environments are in our care. They all deserve our love, whether artifactals, riders, allies, sacramentals, or electro-elementals. We are a contributing factor to their well-being and evolution, sometimes the most powerful factor. It is our responsibility as human beings not to diminish them, burden them with negativity, or disconnect them from their natural surroundings or from their evolutionary drive. We are partners in revealing and manifesting the sacredness that is within all creation. We are roomies in the university of Gaian life and spiritual evolution.

FIELD NOTE 20:
CYBERSPACE, ROBOTS, AND AI, OH MY!

The suggestions I presented in the previous Field Note for working with techno-elementals applies to all our artifacts, electronic or not. The use of electricity, however, has brought into existence a whole new level of artifacts in the form of digital technology, presenting us with a new realm of consciousness and experience in the form of cyberspace, as well as with the development of robots and artificial intelligences which some feel may even replace our own.

As far as I've been able to determine, the word "cyberspace" was coined by the science fiction writer, William Gibson, the author of Neuromancer and other books in what has come to be known as the "cyberpunk" genre. It refers to the psychological space created by interfacing with a computer. Cyberspace exists as a virtual reality brought into being by computer-moderated interactions; in this sense, it is a real "place" I go to when I teach my online classes or use Google to give me information. But in many ways, it is also an imaginative space, much like that created when you read a novel. It has no tangible, material existence in the physical world, other than as a series of ones and zeros in computer servers.

In an interesting way, cyberspace is a non-material reality that mimics many of the characteristics of the actual subtle environment and realms that surround us. For example, in the subtle dimensions, time and space do not function as they do for us here in the physical realms. I may have a close friend who lives three thousand miles away, but though separated by physical distance, I can attune to him, forming a loving resonance, and in so doing, we can be as close energetically as if we were standing side by side. We are in each other's presence though our bodies are mile apart.

Now, with a smartphone in my pocket, I can connect to anyone anywhere on earth who is also part of the Internet or part of a telephonic communications grid. I can Facetime my friend who is three thousand miles away, and we can see each other and talk over our smartphones just as if we were in the same room.

Cyberspace, like the telegraph, the telephone, television, the railroad, air travel, and automobiles, frees us from constraints of time and space in ways that would have seemed magical to our ancestors. This cannot help but have an effect on the consciousness of modern humanity. It enables us to inhabit the world differently than we would have a hundred, two hundred, or a thousand years ago. The world, as experienced by mystics and psychics, has always been profoundly interconnected, but now, through our technology, nearly everyone can experience this in a digital way. This goes beyond the effect of any particular techno-elemental, and I will explore this more fully in the next Field Note.

Returning to cyberspace, though, some years ago, my friend and colleague John Matthews, a world-renowned scholar of the Arthurian mythos and of Celtic shamanism, did some research into this digital domain as a new kind of subtle realm in formation. Though our techniques are different, we both journeyed into cyberspace in the same fashion that we would journey into the subtle environment, and we both discovered, certainly to my surprise and I think to John's as well, that there was an actual, objective subtle domain coming into existence. It is not well-formed—or at least wasn't at that time back in the early years of the Twenty-First century. Here is a comment John sent to me: "When I journeyed there, I saw a landscape marked out in a grid, rather as in the movie *Tron*. When I looked at the shape of a hill of valley it became a hill or valley, when I looked away, I felt it returned to its unformed state. It struck me what a perfect metaphor for the inner realms cyberspace is. It does not have a physical reality, yet it exists, and is in part created by us in collaboration with the Universe."

At another time he wrote, "In one of my classes on Shamanism, I taught people to journey through their computer screens into a new area of the other world. This was described by my allies as 'work in progress'. They told me that journeying into cyberspace was actually creating a new area within the subtle worlds."

My experience was similar. When I looked to see if there were any "cyber-elementals," however, beings uniquely connected with cyberspace, I could not discern any. What I did tune into were subtle allies that normally associate with human beings, which makes sense, given that cyberspace is in many ways a projection of human consciousness. I did become aware over time of angelic presences overlighting this development, though I would not say that I ever perceived something like a singular "Angel" or "Deva" of cyberspace (which doesn't mean such a Being may not exist, of course).

However, the most important aspect of cyberspace was something I discovered quite by accident in the early Nineties when personal computers were still something of a novelty. As an experiment, I began teaching some of my classes online over the Internet. Being partly deaf, this was actually easier for me in some ways since all the class interactions were done in writing. Still, I wasn't at all sure it would work. Although my hearing (or lack thereof) could give me some problems in my face-to-face classes, it was more than compensated by the field of subtle energy and resonance we could build together. In fact, the subtle energy transmissions between me and the participants was one of the important features of these classes. I had no idea if this could be replicated online.

As it turned out, the subtle field generated between me and my online students turned out to be as strong, and at times stronger, than that manifested in classes where we were altogether in the same room. I found that cyberspace could be a powerful conductor of subtle energies, which, when I thought about it, made sense given that it was fundamentally a mental and imaginal realm itself. Also, there were none of the distractions that could arise in physical space. A subtle field could manifest, for instance, unimpeded by personality reactions to what someone else looked like or what their voice sounded like!

As a result of this experience, I began to use cyberspace as a conduit for blessings. I work on the computer nearly every day, writing and teaching classes. When I log on and the digital connections are made between my computer and the Internet, I imagine that I'm entering a space shared by millions of other people. I connect to spiritual allies and ask that my presence in cyberspace provide an opening for blessing to flow to whomever or wherever it can do the most good.

In effect, I am making use of the resonance created by countless people doing the same thing at the same time to create a link through which blessings may pass. This is a simple practice that anyone can do, turning the computer into a spiritual tool. (The same can be true when using a smartphone. Any digital device that connects us to the "space of connection" that is cyberspace can be used in this way as a portal for blessing.)

Much is in the news these days about the accelerating development of robots and of artificial intelligence. My children built and played with simple electronic robots when they were younger, but these were no different as artifacts from any other electrical or mechanical device in our household. I have had no opportunity to investigate more sophisticated robots or artificial intelligences, so I do not know what their subtle aspects might be like. If I were to speculate, I would imagine they could attract complex elementals and riders, but otherwise, they would essentially be like the machines we already know. However, an AI that can learn and develop in ways that transcend and modify its programming may generate a subtle field capable of supporting a complex consciousness. Then one has to think of when an intelligence crosses a boundary of evolution and no longer is "artificial." Could an advanced digital organism embody a soul or a spiritual intelligence? From what I know of the subtle realms and the dynamics of subtle energies, I would say this is possible, but I would also surmise that it would take greater knowledge and skill—and wisdom and love—than modern cyberneticists and robotics engineers currently have, especially given the materialistic mind-set of our society.

This is a whole, wide field for subtle research, far beyond what I can give to it. My experience with the digital world is largely limited to my computer and my smartphone, and as artifacts, they possess the same techno-elementals and electro-elementals as all the other human-made objects in my environment. Beyond this, the subtle realms aspects of digital technology have not been the focus of my work. I am hopeful that others with more experience and skill in this area than I have will be inspired to explore the subtle life associated with these emerging new dimensions in our world.

There is, however, one thing that is clear to me. As our technology becomes ever more complex and sophisticated in augmenting and mimicking human capabilities, it is increasingly important to affirm our human wholeness. Machines can already out-perform what our muscles can do, and computers can do mental tasks far faster and more accurately than we can. However, none of our technologies contain the complexity of the human soul nor our empathic and loving ability to create wholeness.

Throughout our history, we have been shaped by our tools. Now, though, our digital tools—our computers, robots, and artificial intelligences—have a power to shape us and our evolution in unprecedented ways. They shape our imagination about ourselves and who we are. For instance, our brains are far more sophisticated than any computer, yet we have developed the habit of talking about ourselves as being "programmed" to do this or that as if we were something manufactured by IBM. We limit our humanity by defining ourselves in terms of our tools.

There are even movements to "upload" our consciousnesses into computers, to leave the "meat world" behind. Those who promote this, part of a "trans-humanity" movement, have decided that as an organic being, humanity is too weak, too limited; our hope to evolve into something better lies in turning ourselves into digital beings—in a sense, becoming techno-elementals ourselves.

Our tools have always had a capacity to seduce us, and none more powerfully than the digital technologies that increasingly fill our world. However, the relationship we need with our technology and with the subtle organisms that are part of it, the techno-elementals, is not to become like them but to be even more clear in standing in who and what we are as whole human beings. We cannot be symbiotic partners if we don't keep up our end of the partnership. And partnership, not dominance, is what subtle life is all about.

FIELD NOTE 21: PARTNERSHIP

I want to emphasize here what I said in the introduction, that this is a very experimental, exploratory area for me. I don't consider myself an expert. The realm of techno-elementals is complex and vast, just as the organic, biological realm is. Further, the impact and influence of techno-elementals, particularly of the electronic and digital variety, are still unfolding. In the context of all of human evolution, this is a very early encounter indeed.

But one thing seems very clear to me. We will make little progress with attitudes that pit the techno-world against the natural world, seeing one as better than the other. There is really only one world with many different parts and elements that exist in a complex ecology. The technological world may be humanly created but it doesn't exist in a vacuum.

For many of us, the technological world is our everyday equivalent of the forests and fields, rivers and mountains of our ancestors. It is an ecology in which new kinds of shamanism, new kinds of spirituality, new kinds of inner work are both open to us and needed to form alliances and partnerships. We need to integrate with the subtle lives we have drawn into our human world and to minimize the negative effects that can be there where that integration is lacking. So, it behooves us, I feel, to stop erecting in our thinking divisions that separate the natural from the technological and to begin thinking of ways of touching the deeper, spiritual aspects of the techno-world that is arising around us.

The good news is that we are fully capable of doing that. It may just require a shift in our thinking, a reframing of our worldview. This is not always a simple task, but it is a doable one.

A step is to begin appreciating, honoring, and loving the technological things in our lives and seeing them as points of connection with lives that are very different from our own but still part of the Sacred. Even if I don't like a particular piece of technology and what it does, I can still love the sacredness within it or the living techno-elemental force with which it is connected.

I can also explore new forms of spiritual practice. If I am oriented to a shamanic approach, I can explore seeking technological allies, as well as the more familiar ones associated with the natural world. Why couldn't a television, a computer, or a Harley-Davidson be a "power creature" for me?

In situations where I might call upon the energies and forces of spiritual allies, might I not include the spirit of the technological things around me in that invocation? The techno-elemental of my phone or my printer, my car or my dishwasher might be able to help me, too. I know of many people for whom this has been the case.

I can practice my own methods of attunement and integration with the larger world of spirit and from that attunement reach out to offer blessing to the machinery around me. I can appreciate a gadget not only for what it does but just for the sake of its being.

I can refuse to see my world divided into artificial things and natural things but instead insist that my consciousness and attitudes project a field of unity and integration that draws these two aspects of nature into a closer oneness.

To be a good partner, I want to be clear and strong in the spiritual presence of my own humanity, my own personhood. If elementals are watching and learning, then let me be a good example for them of what a human being is.

This is an evolving area of partnership. We can serve it by no longer seeing the technological arena as bereft of spirit, but instead by calling that area to acknowledge and align with the sacredness from which we all emerge. It is the techno-elementals, who are spiritual beings in their own right, who have a power to connect our technology with a larger wholeness, if we can acknowledge them and work with them as partners.

The nature and function of techno-elementals is a rich area of spiritual investigation. There is much more to it than I have put into this book. My purpose here has been to keep it simple, even though it may not have seemed that way at times! Basically, there have been just two ideas I've wanted to communicate to you. The first is that techno-elementals exist and that our artifacts, our built world, is an environment filled with subtle life and spiritual forces. The second is that this world needs us and depends on us. It needs our partnership to rebuild the bridge of communion, communication, and wholeness. We meet that need with our acknowledgement, our appreciation, and our love. These three are the basis on which all other work with techno-elementals is based, just as they are the foundation for doing work with any subtle organism.

We in the modern world have traveled a long way in consciousness from talisman to tech, from a shamanic awareness of the world in which everything is alive to a technological perspective in which the cosmos is unliving matter meant to be subdued by human ingenuity and tools. Even as human society, in the face of environmental difficulties and challenges, is learning to recover an ecological perspective, so we are also at a time when we need to recover our vision and awareness of being part of a living, interconnected universe and in so doing re-kindle our own incarnate soul presence. Understanding the challenge of the techno-elementals is an important step in that direction.

May you take that step with blessing, for yourself and for everything in your world.

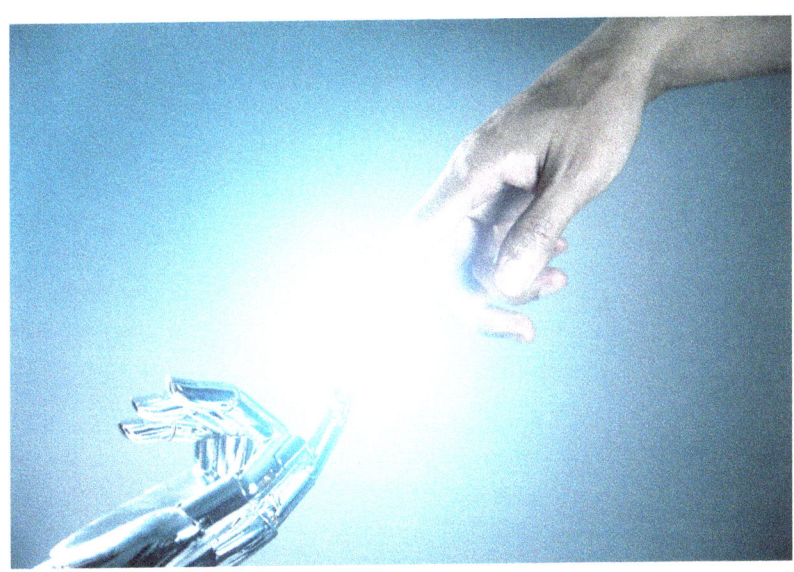

EXERCISES

Generally speaking, each time we hold or use an artifact, or enter a building or a room, or gaze upon something someone has created, we have an opportunity to engage with techno-elementals. The simplest way to do so is to acknowledge and affirm their presence and their life as fellow evolving beings, to appreciate them for what they are and what they do—for the sacredness within them—and to send them love and blessing in whatever manner is appropriate. In other words, be aware that you are always in the midst of life and honor it accordingly.

When you are in a building or in your own home, a simple approach is to attune to an angel or Deva overlighting that building, or your home, and, after greeting it with appreciation and love, ask it to bless all the subtle lives—and the physical ones, too—that are within its field of awareness, which generally will mean within that structure. When you make connection in your own mind between the techno-elementals and the overlighting angelic or Devic intelligence, it adds your energy to the connections that are already there and strengthens them.

If you would like to do something more specific to engage with the techno-elementals of your world, here are two fundamental exercises—Touch of Love and Grail Space—to get you started.

TOUCH OF LOVE EXERCISE

This is an exercise to directly bless a specific object and the techno-elementals within and around it.

- Fill yourself with a felt sense of lovingness. You might imagine, for instance, your heart overflowing with love or your spine glowing with love. Express the highest form of love that you can authentically feel in your whole being—body, mind, heart, energy, and soul—right now.
- Feel this love flowing out from the core of your being, down your arms and into your hands. Feel this love pooling in your fingertips.
- Reach out and touch something. As you do so, feel the love in your fingertips overflowing. In this Touch of Love, you do not take anything into yourself. You do not really project it into anything, either. You simply let it pool in your fingertips and overflow, allowing that which you touch to absorb it in its own way.
- Visualize this overflowing love entering and blessing the subtle life within that which you are touching. In your mind and heart, ask that it be nourishing and empowering to the techno-elementals associated with that which you are touching.
- As love flows through your touch, it also stirs and flows and circulates through your own being, bringing love to all parts of yourself just as you are bringing it to the things you touch.
- Likewise, as love flows through your touch, it also stirs and flows and circulates through your environment, rippling out in waves from the things you touch, from the techno-elemental life under your fingers to other techno-elemental and subtle lives in your surroundings, expanding the influence of your loving touch.
- When you feel finished, just remove your fingers and allow the love to be absorbed into all parts of your body.

GRAIL SPACE EXERCISE

Introduction

I use the term "Grail Space" to mean any space or field of subtle energies that holds sacredness, just as in legend the Holy Grail held the transformative blood of Christ. Sacredness in this instance manifests as the incarnational consciousness and process that brings creation into being and sustains it in its unfoldment

We live in Grail Space. The entire cosmos is the primal Grail Space holding the sacredness of the Generative Mystery which I call the Sacred. But this primal Grail Space can be accentuated in local space at any time that we invoke the presence and flow of sacredness by honoring the incarnational process through which it manifests.

The practice of creating a local Grail space is one of the principle practices of Incarnational Spirituality. It consists of standing in our own Sovereignty and Self-Light and engaging the local environment around us to evoke more fully the Life and Light that flows from the primal Grail Space, i.e. from the Sacred itself. Fundamentally, this is a practice of connecting through Presence and love with everything around us. It is an act of honoring and relating to our environment, inviting the life within it to respond energetically and express its own Grail capacities. It is the act of mutual holding that turns the environment, with ourselves in it, into a Grail in which sacredness may shine forth.

The creation of Grail Space is a reciprocal act, not something we do to anything else. It is an act of extending an invitation, allowing the environment to respond as fully as it can in the moment. Grail Space is born of relationship and mutual engagement based on honoring the sovereignty and identity of all involved.

Creating Grail Space is really a simple process, but I break it down into a number of steps just so you can get a sense of the procedure. To read it, it can seem like a lot, but it's really a very fast, simple process. The main difference between this technique and simply sending love into your environment is the act of honoring and connecting with the identity of everything about you in a partnership. It is not you doing something to the things in your environment. It is you joining with them in collaboration to create a mutually beneficial space or field into which sacredness may be invoked.

One way to think of this is as if your environment is alive with people, and you are joining hands with them to form a great circle. This circle creates the Grail Space, and into it sacredness is invoked.

The Exercise

- Begin by standing in your own Sovereignty, in the felt sense of your unique identity and your connection to your soul and to the sacred. If you wish, you can imagine this Sovereignty as a "spine" of Light within you, an axis around which your physical and subtle bodies develop and align.
- Imagine this spine of Light becoming brighter and brighter as it unfolds from the love within your Soul and within the Sacred of which it is a part. As this Light becomes brighter within you, it expands and enfolds you.
- Imagine yourself standing in an oval of Light emanating from your "spine" of Sovereignty and individuality, an oval that surrounds you on all sides, top and bottom, connecting you with the energies of the world. It forms and radiates from you as a personal Grail, an incarnational field holding sacredness.
- Everything in your immediate environment is an expression of the Sacred. Everything you see participates in the primal Grail Space. Everything has within itself a "spine" of incarnational intent and Light, its own form of Sovereignty and identity, its own purpose and evolutionary spirit. Imagine yourself surrounded with a multitude of "grails of Light" emanating from everything in the space around you. In your heart, acknowledge and give honor to the presence of all these "spines" or "grails" of incarnational and sacred Light.
- Imagine the aura of your internal, personal Grail of sacredness and incarnational Light expanding into the room, joining in love with the myriad multitude of Lights all around you, inviting

them into an alliance and collaboration with you. Feel your Light augmenting and blending with the Lights around you, feel their Lights blending with and augmenting your own. You are forming a subtle partnership with your environment and everything seen and unseen within it. Feel this partnership turning your immediate, local environment into a Grail that you and all the things around you collaborate to create, a Grail you share.
- The felt sense of this partnership and the field of reciprocal energy that generates it is the Grail Space. It is a field of collaborative partnership and support in the incarnational process with everything around you in your local space, a partnership and fellowship that can receive and hold a Presence of sacredness, a presence of Gaia.
- Standing in this Grail Space, acknowledge this Presence of sacredness heightened in yourself and your environment. Imagine it being held in this space, doing whatever it needs to do to foster wholeness and well-being within your surroundings and then overflowing into the larger world beyond, a source of energy, blessing, love, and life.
- Stay in this Grail Space as long as feels comfortable. When you feel tired or restless, simply draw your Self-Light back into yourself, giving thanks to your energy partners for their participation. Imagine their incarnational light moving back into themselves as well, knowing the environment you share will resonate with the Light and Presence you have collectively invoked for as long as it is able.
- Stand in your Sovereignty, acknowledging your wholeness your integrity, your identity, and your connection to the Sacred. Then go about your daily affairs.

If you would like to explore other exercises for working with subtle energies and subtle beings, please see my book, *Working with Subtle Energies*. If you would like information about the principles of Incarnational Spirituality, please see my book, *Journey into Fire*. In addition, the Lorian Association offers classes and workshops in these topics. For information, please see our website, Lorian.org.

www.ingramcontent.com/pod-product-compliance
Lightning Source LLC
Chambersburg PA
CBHW040313170426
43195CB00020B/2953